SUPPORT FOR THE FALLACY OF AFFINITY

"*The Fallacy of Affinity* is an impassioned plea written by a man with a pastor's heart to call attention to a 'final frontier' which the Church has failed to journey towards, much less cross. This frontier of cross-cultural integrated worship is shown to be not just some warm and fuzzy glorious eschatological destiny but as a present ecclesiological scriptural imperative. For churches willing to rise to the challenge this may mean starting with actively seeking integration with previously ignored constituencies. For others with outwardly integrated fellowships, it will mean intentional penetration past the surface comfort zone of the individual and into the zone of vulnerability and trust. For all, the goal is to continually live the demanding Kingdom life of reconciliation NOW! Written in a very direct conversational style, I hope it will be read widely by Christians who are seeking biblical guidance for a model of multicultural worship, but especially by church leaders who have the responsibility to equip God's people for the ONE worship of the ONE Lord."

Dr. Edwin Chan
Head of Epidemiology, Singapore Clinical Research Institute
Associate Professor, Duke-National University of Singapore,
Graduate Medical School

"The Bible is the starting place for exposing *The Fallacy of Affinity*. With incisive Biblical interpretation and application, my long time friend, Barron Witherspoon, has delivered a must read for the serious thinking Christian of today, who truly wants to see the reality of every "nation, tribe, people and language...standing before the throne, and before the Lamb" in worship together. As the author points out, if that's what Heaven will be like, why don't we begin practicing it on earth? With keen personal insights and an intentional life of integrity, Barron personally demonstrates what it is to really live out the Christian life with integrity and obedience to God. He not only illustrates from his own life experiences, he also gives a well thought out strategy for tearing down the walls of affinity that hinder the effective movement of God through His people. It has been said that the "heart of the problem is the problem of the heart." Like a masterful surgeon, the author probes into the depths of our hearts and offers strategic steps to ridding us of our clogged, spiritual arteries. Then he offers a rehab process for complete healing by God's Spirit. May the Lord use this work of love and life testimony to encourage God's people to cross cultural worship as the new norm, rather than the exception."

Dr. Stephen P. Davis
Executive Director
State Convention of Baptists in Indiana

"What a thrill to be a part of this journey from prejudice to true enlightenment. Barron Witherspoon introduces us to his life, and passion. He documents his insight informatively, yet the book is more than a motivational treatise. It is a beacon of light interspersed with a lifetime of testimonies of changed lives, families, churches and communities. With the teaching of the Bible he shares what is true and clearly articulates how we resolve *The Fallacy of Affinity*."

R. Kirby Lancaster, M.D.

"Barron Witherspoon is one of the finest and most godly men I have ever had the privilege to pastor. His commitment to see the church worship as one body of people represents the heart of Jesus and the New Testament church. Cross-cultural worship can occur and should occur in the church. Let this book help you adjust your thinking and your church towards worshipping as one. Read this book. Share it with others."

Dr. Ronnie W. Floyd, Senior Pastor,
First Baptist Church of Springdale and The Church at Pinnacle Hills, Arkansas

"This book comes from the heart of a man whose desire is to follow the command of Jesus Christ to 'love the Lord' and to love 'thy neighbor as thyself'. The love for his neighbor has been modeled to me personally to promote cross-cultural worship. This love is now expressed with eloquence in a biblically thorough and thought-provoking case for breaking down the wall of spiritual segregation that is a 'plank in the eye' of today's churches. Witherspoon puts a spotlight on reconciliation, its biblical mandate, and provides practical steps for implementing cross-cultural worship. The book is a powerful and Spirit-filled work that is overdue. I pray its message will reach the hearts, souls, minds, and hands of leaders and laypersons to move past fear and prejudice, and to truly love thy neighbor."

Dr. Curtis R. Taylor,
Professor, University of Florida

"I am privileged to say that Barron Witherspoon is my friend. Our friendship began more than fifteen years ago and we knew very early that God had allowed it for a purpose only He could know. The development of his book *The Fallacy of Affinity* was taking place through those years. Our partnership in ministry for the cause of Christ continues today. This book is biblically sound, culturally relevant, and addresses in a comprehensive way an issue the church must face. I pray the content will expose the need for church leaders and churches to strive for cross-cultural worship and find the value, joy, and freedom in it."

Rev. Brent Jones, Senior Pastor
Forestville Baptist Church, Cincinnati, Ohio

"*The Fallacy of Affinity* propels the conversation of race relations in the body of Christ. Barron is honest and thorough in his effort to remind us all of the necessity of unity in worship and praxis regardless of race, ethnicity, or gender. This is a must read for believers who truly have a heart to see the world from a Kingdom perspective."

Delesslyn Audra Kennebrew, J.D., M.Div.
President/CEO, Spirited Concepts Consulting Network LLC

"Barron Witherspoon has used his eloquent style of storytelling to present a thorny issue with persuasive impact requiring the reader to seriously consider the importance and benefit of cross cultural worship in churches across America and the world. I had the privilege to work alongside my brother as a fellow deacon and elder at the International Baptist Church of Singapore and was blessed to have learnt much from him on the need and benefits that come from investing time in people from all races and cultures. I can testify to the results achieved when God used Barron to transform IBC from a fractious group split on racial lines into a body that has genuine concern and love for others of different races, color and nationalities. The model for the cross cultural church has its challenges which can be mitigated with the 12 points advocated by Barron and when overcome will become a body that is mandated by God and pleasing in His sight."

Andrew Hanam, Advocate & Solicitor
Republic of Singapore

THE FALLACY OF AFFINITY

A Case for Cross-Cultural Worship

By
Barron Witherspoon, Sr.

Grace and Peace

First published by Dog Ear Publishing
4010 W. 86th Street, Ste H
Indianapolis, IN 46268
www.dogearpublishing.net

dog ear
PUBLISHING

ISBN: 978-160844-738-1

This book is printed on acid-free paper.

Printed in the United States of America

ACKNOWLEDGEMENTS

I dedicate this work first to the memory of my mother, Thelma Juanita Witherspoon-Claiborne, who has gone home to be with the Lord. She taught me many life lessons including the value of building cross-cultural relationships. Second, I dedicate this work to Karen, Briana, Barron Jr, Florence, Ronald, George, Gardell, and Gregory for being present in some combination at every milestone of my life. Third, I dedicate this work to every mentor, colleague, instructor and friend who has invested in my development as a leader at home, at church, at work, at school or at any other point of interest or action in my life. Finally and with greatest emphasis – I dedicate this work to my Savior and Lord Jesus Christ and I pray He would be pleased with the meditations of my heart and the work of my hands.

Barron Witherspoon, Sr.

TABLE OF CONTENTS

PART IV. THE CROSS-CULTURAL EXPERIENCE

PART V. THEN GOD DELIVERED

PART VI. PRINCIPLES FOR APPLICATION

FOREWORD

Readers customarily skip the foreword. Often it is misspelled "forward" because people flip pages into the book being anxious to see immediately what the author has to say. But you will actually find the word "forward" not here but in the conclusion as the author's way of encouraging the readers to act upon his challenge of implementing cross- or multi-cultural worship in churches today.

In the 1960s, theological discussions on the church and her mission were dominated by the mantra of church growth—homogeneous church groups attract more people and result in exponential growth. With Fuller Seminary as its seedbed and Dr. Donald MacGavran as its main guru ably fortified by seminal research exponents Ralph Winter and Peter Wagner, the movement became the mission banner for the decades that follow. Arguably it yielded the numbers and proved effective. But some say it fostered ethnic and economic divides and furthered prevailing social inequities.

Indeed it is also noteworthy that in 1962 Marshall McLuhan popularized the phrase "global village" to highlight the influence of technology and travel that made the globe smaller. Economists and social scientists in the 60s also began using "globalization" to describe the process of network integration of communication, technology, trade and travel. Then in 2005, Thomas L. Friedman wrote the bestseller The World Is Flat to extol the inevitability and reality of global interaction and integration. Given these, homogeneity and affinity should have become anachronistic.

Today, church health has replaced church growth as the ideal alternative goal for mission. *The Fallacy of Affinity* is Barron Witherspoon's call to unlearn homogeneity as a primary strategy for church growth. He argues that "racial and ethnic reconciliation is the last enduring frontier left for the church to address and tackle." Deal with race and ethnicity and the related barriers of age, class and gender will follow suit toward resolution processes. Using biblical exegesis enhanced by considerable global and multi-cultural personal experience, professional tools and ministry engagement, the author presents a formidable challenge for action. With enough data and processing suggestions, he presents the guidelines for implementation. His examples are well-documented and practical.

Among the many examples cited by Witherspoon, the International Baptist Church of Singapore stands out as a quintessential test case for the principles advocated in the book. Although our ministry partnership record may be brief, that experience, more precisely, that struggle gives me basis for an unreserved affirmation that Barron Witherspoon knows his stuff and he should be heard.

I end by citing where the author began. In John's vision of worship in heaven, he saw a great and innumerable multitude from every nation, tribe, people and language. United but with their distinct ethnic identities intact, they worship the Lamb (Revelation 7:9). If that is what eternity is like, then cross- and multi-cultural worship is God's will even now for the church on earth.

"Thy will be done on earth as it is in heaven."

Luis L. Pantoja, Jr., ThD.
Greenhills Christian Fellowship
Pasig City, Philippines

INTRODUCTION

This book is the product of ten years of personal research and practical application. In the summer of 1998, while attending seminary, I became thoroughly engulfed in the reality of the Church's unequivocal failure to truly embrace cross-cultural worship. This realization has occupied my most intense thought from that long ago summer to the moment this manuscript went to press.

While I am humbled and encouraged by the prospect that some non-Christians would read this book, it is written to Christians. The sentiments contained here are meant to stimulate the entire body of born-again believers toward the spiritual journey I have traveled over these past several years.

From academic research, personal experience and extended practical application I have reached a startling, singular conclusion—any ministry that does not have a clear and compelling objective to enable cross-cultural worship among the fellowship of believers is working against God's plan for His Church. Why do I say this? I say it because unlike many faiths, Christians can know through the Holy Bible God's plan for eternity. In other words, we know the "end game" because the Bible describes it for us. If we know the end game, that is, if we know what heaven will be like, then why would we operate God's Church as though we didn't have that knowledge?

You see, the fact is God has presented us a clear picture of heaven. It is a heaven where God's people will be unified with Him on one accord and worshipping Him continually in spirit and in truth. The Bible does not offer us many heavens with differing styles of worship based upon human affinities. Instead, we are presented with the undeniable prospect of one heaven, occupied by one people, focused upon one God. You may be thinking, at this time, "I'm tracking with you so far." Good, but here is the issue that is yet unresolved—why is the Church still segregated along well-preserved racial and socio-economic lines? Not only that, but why is the Church contented to operate this way when we already know these distinctions will definitely not exist in heaven? There, I've said it. This is the nagging line of questions that have compelled me to write to you—The Church. Are you still tracking with me?

By now, you are probably thinking about your own Church. Maybe you are mentally examining its racial and economic stratification and composition. No doubt, some readers will be impressed by the mixture in their congregations. Others may be troubled by the stark lack of diversity in their church body. Hopefully, you are at least tuning into the possibility that the Church can and should be doing more to bring today's Sunday morning worship experience more into harmony with the Biblical end game for corporate worship.

In the book we will carefully examine God's plan for corporate worship. It is a plan of cross-cultural worship akin to the miracle of Pentecost when the Spirit of God moved powerfully among the people and broke through the perceived barriers of people's ethnic and linguistic affinities. It is a glorious vision of God's people at our individual and collective best with each and all of us in perfect, eternal harmony with the will of God.

In the summer of 1998 a fire was kindled in my heart toward the question of cross-cultural worship and its centrality in the Christian experience God has planned for His Church. I read, again, the entire scripture from Genesis chapter one to Revelation chapter twenty two. In so doing, I was struck by the undeniable emphasis placed on cross-cultural worship in the New Testament. I found passage after passage directly addressing this theme. Through it all I returned to the conclusion—any ministry that does not have a clear and compelling objective to enable cross-cultural worship among the fellowship of believers is working against God's plan for His Church. Consider the words of the apostle John who is often remembered as John the

Revelator (or Revealer) because of his picturesque vision of the end times as revealed to him by God and captured for us in the Book of Revelation.

The apostle John, in his vivid description of heaven, declares, "And I saw a new heaven and a new earth: for the first heaven and the first earth were passed away; and there was no more sea. And I saw the holy city, New Jerusalem, coming down from God out of heaven, prepared as a bride adorned for her husband."[1] These first two verses of Revelation chapter 21 give us a profound back drop for understanding what heaven will be for the redeemed. He mentions, in verse 2 a specific location called New Jerusalem. This is the dwelling place of God's people in eternity. The Revelator goes on to say, "And I heard a great voice out of heaven saying, the tabernacle of God is with men, and He will dwell with them, and they shall be His people, and God himself shall be with them, and be their God."[2] There is only one city described—New Jerusalem. The apostle John did not see a group of white believers in a New York, a group of black believers in a New Atlanta, or a group of Hispanic believers in a New Miami. He sees only one group of believers, one tabernacle, and one God for them all. This is the end game of corporate worship. Nothing we can do will alter this eventual outcome. This is where God is taking His Church. Why should any ministry strive against this direction by allowing worldly divisions to persist unchecked and unchallenged in the Church? Let us explore these nagging questions together.

THE CHURCH MUST MOVE

The modern Church must move with intent toward cross-cultural worship. Continuing to deny the challenge won't make it go away. Remember, the end game is already established. Acknowledging the challenge, but failing to address it is, at worst, deceptive or spiritually irresponsible and, at best, cowardly or intellectually dishonest. I have never heard so many excuses among Christian leaders and workers as I get when probing their inaction on this critical issue. I will return to the matter of excuses later. For now, let me say making excuses or doing nothing hardly seem to be the reasonable course when the facts are presented. So let us get into the facts without delay.

The Biblical Mandate

The Church must move with intent toward cross-cultural worship because there is a clear and continuous Biblical mandate to do so. The New Testament is replete with support for a determined focus on cross-cultural worship in the body of Christ. In making this point, scripture addresses the toughest issue or barrier in bringing cross-cultural worship to life—racial reconciliation. You see, God's great master plan and eternal purpose for His Church is to restore our unconditional worship of Him alone. His plan is to reconcile us to Himself.

Years ago, when I started this journey of understanding cross-cultural worship, I read everything I could find on the subject. In addition to scriptural references, I found and read thousands of pages on the topic. One book, popular at the time, was written by Raleigh

Washington and Glen Kehrein. They shared some great insights by showing how the Bible addresses the issue of racial reconciliation. It should be noted, their testimony was a case study in racial reconciliation—one was African American and the other was Caucasian American. Together, they started a ministry at the Church of the Rock in Chicago, Illinois. This ministry was an intentional and successful effort toward cross-cultural worship. Their book, *Breaking Down Walls*, chronicled some of the key scriptural texts supporting Christian involvement in racial reconciliation.

Among the most important passages are Christ's own words in Matthew 22.[3] A Pharisee asked, "Master, which is the great commandment in the law?" The Lord answered, "Thou shalt love the Lord thy God with all thy heart, and with all thy soul, and with all thy mind (verse 37)." In this statement Christ addresses the first-order need of reconciliation: our need to be reconciled to God.

The Lord goes on, in verse 39 to declare a second commandment which is "like unto [the first]", specifically, "thou shalt love thy neighbor as thyself (verse 39)." This addresses the second-order need of reconciliation: our need to be reconciled to each other. Herein is the rub. Most of us in the Church can readily accept, even practice, the Biblical imperative to love the Lord with all our heart, soul and mind. We vigorously pursue this quest and some of us are willing to die for this cause—the cause of expressing our love for God. Daniel and Joshua, in the Old Testament, were willing to die for this cause, as were Paul and Peter in the New Testament. Maybe you are willing to die for it.

However, too many of us are unwilling to die for the cause of loving our neighbors. Sadly, most don't even recognize this is part and parcel of God's plan for His Church. We often fail to realize it is required, according to Matthew 22:39, that we love our neighbor "like" we love our God! Who among us are willing to die for the cause of expressing this Christian love toward our neighbor, our brothers and sisters in Christ? Are you?

Another key scripture is found in 2 Corinthians 5:17-21 where Paul summarizes the imperative nature of the reconciliation ministry for "all" brethren. The Apostle Paul states, "Therefore if any man be in Christ, he is a new creature: old things are passed away; behold, all things are become new." What a revolutionary thought—all things are become new. Paul goes on to explain this powerful thought in verse 18 when he says, "And all things are of God, who has reconciled us to himself by Jesus Christ, and hath given to us the ministry of reconciliation; . . ., that God was in Christ, reconciling the world unto himself, not imputing their trespasses unto them; and hath committed unto us the word of reconciliation. . .we pray you in Christ's stead, be ye reconciled to God."

Do you see what has happened? We, the Church, have been given the ministry of reconciliation. That is, we are an extension of Christ's ministry of reconciliation. We are now responsible, as the body of Christ, to fully engage the work of personally being reconciled to God and enabling others to be reconciled to God. This important passage underscores the church's role in bringing reconciliation to life. Now let me connect this to the passage in Matthew 22. You see, in order to truly love our neighbor as we love ourselves (Matthew 22:39) we must be likewise engaged in reconciling our neighbors and ourselves to God.

Are you still tracking with me? Good. I really want you to catch the full force of this next passage. Let me give you a third scripture found in chapter 2 of Paul's letter to the church at Ephesus, "For he is our peace, who hath made both [Jew and Gentile] one, and hath broken down the middle wall of partition between us: . . . for to make in himself of twain one new man. . . . that he might reconcile both unto God in one body by the cross, having slain the enmity thereby."[4]

Earlier I said in order to truly love our neighbor as ourselves we must be likewise engaged in reconciling our neighbors and ourselves to God. To do this—to truly love our neighbors—we must come to realize our role in picking up the mantle of Christ's ministry of reconciliation. But who is our neighbor? Our neighbors are those closest to us. In the context of Ephesians 2, Jews and Gentiles are "neighbors." Keep in mind, this letter is written to the Church at Ephesus, not to non-Christians.[5] It was a cross-cultural church comprised of both Jews and Gentiles. By the way, you couldn't get any more culturally distinctive—in the mind of a Jew, a Gentile was a cultural opposite. Yet, the Apostle Paul completely transforms this cultural distinctive into a cultural indistinctive.

He says Christ has made in himself of twain (two) one new man! How can this be?

It can be because Jesus Christ broke down the middle wall of partition between us. This is a reference to the wall or curtain in the Temple that separated the court of the Gentiles from the Court of the Jews. No Gentile was permitted to enter beyond this point in the temple at Jerusalem. If they went beyond this point, they did so at their own peril—yes they could be killed for doing so. What's the big deal about entering into the Temple? The Temple is where the glory of God would come and dwell among the people. In this construct, the Gentiles were separated not only from the Jewish people, but separated from God.

So what does all this mean? It means that Jesus Christ, by breaking down this wall, established a new construct. This new construct was one of "cross-cultural worship" where a cultural distinctive did not form a basis for who could enter the presence of God. Beyond that, it meant that a new man or "new creature" would emerge who was neither Jew nor Gentile. This new man would later be called "Christian" by the Church at Antioch—the first place the disciples were called by this name.[6] Now let me connect this passage from Ephesians to the earlier passages in Matthew and 2 Corinthians. In order to truly love our neighbor as ourselves we must likewise be engaged in reconciling ourselves and our neighbors to God and realizing that our neighbors and we are one in Jesus Christ.

These three passages combine to form a powerful Biblical mandate for Christians to enable cross-cultural worship through the ministry of reconciliation given to us by Christ. Now if you are up for it, let's take this a bit deeper. Some might argue they understand there is a mandate, but it is not necessarily their job to work on this "reconciliation stuff." They argue someone else can work on reconciliation and cross-cultural worship. They are having "success" with homogeneous congregations so God must be blessing their ministry. Each minister can choose their own focus areas and it will all be used of God. People don't want to mix across cultures anyway, so why force it? This line of logic ends with a question. Whose role is it to execute the ministry of reconciliation? I believe it is the work of every Christian. What do you think?

Before you answer, let me share a few more points with you. First, Jesus Christ was direct and intentional about enabling cross-cultural worship; second, Jesus Christ commanded His Church to carry out this mandate until He returns; and third, the early church understood this mandate and acted upon it. Let us take each in turn.

Have you ever noticed how much personal effort Christ expended toward cross-cultural worship? I have. In fact, if you read the New Testament carefully you will see Jesus was continually driving this outcome in many aspects of His earthly ministry. Perhaps a few examples will make the point that Jesus was all about cross-cultural worship. To illustrate this point we will highlight the words of Jesus for your reference and consideration. I want to show you how the words of Christ speak directly to cross-cultural worship.

When Jesus assembled his ministry team, the twelve apostles, this was a deliberate effort to enable cross-cultural worship. Though all of them were Jews there are some interesting characteristics among this group. Though most of Jesus' early ministry was among the Jewish people, it is clear He was always setting the stage for followers to understand the universal relevance of his message. In calling His first twelve apostles all seemed "normal" until He called Levi (or Matthew). In Mark's gospel account we read, "And as he passed by, he saw Levi the son of Alpheus sitting at the receipt of custom, and he said unto him, 'Follow me.' And he arose and followed him."[7] Luke's account of this same event describes the apostle as "a publican named Levi."[8] From these parallel passages we confirm that Levi was a publican or tax collector employed by the Romans to collect the tax from a Hebrew community. When Jesus saw him sitting there at the tax table he could have passed Levi by without a word. In fact, this would not only have been normal, it would have been expected of any decent Jew to not even speak to a tax collector. So why did Jesus stop to address Levi?

He addressed Levi because this was part of Jesus' plan to show the power of reaching out across boundaries to embrace people in Christian love and reconciliation. By calling Matthew, Jesus intentionally crossed the line established by Jewish tradition. He paused to acknowledge a publican—one despised by his own people. Can you see Jesus standing in front of Matthew, and in plain view of other passers-by? Jesus already had several apostles on board. I wonder what they thought of his calling Matthew. Knowing what we now know about Peter's firebrand personality, I often wonder specifically what he thought. Of course, Peter had no way of knowing all that Jesus had in store for him and his colleagues. He certainly had no idea God would eventually reveal to him, through a dream, the broader relevance of the gospel to all mankind. Despite this cultural context Jesus extended His call to Matthew.

Notice also the words of Christ when He said, "Follow me" in calling Matthew. These two words showed the power of Christ's love toward humanity. It may seem trite to some, but Jesus knew this was a big deal. Jesus crossed the line of tradition and cultural norms because He wanted Matthew to see the possibilities of eternal life. When Jesus said, "Follow me" it was not a passive invitation to come if you have time or if you can fit it into your schedule. Jesus spoke these words like a command toward Matthew.[9] It is no wonder the Bible says Matthew rose up, left all, and followed him.[10]

Yes, Jesus Christ was personally invested in the work and ministry of reconciliation. I know you may be thinking, but Levi was himself a Jew so this is not really a cross-cultural outreach. Perhaps this next example will help us see the point more clearly. In John chapter 4, the Apostle John relates the story of Jesus' encounter with the Samaritan woman at Jacob's well. Here again, it is important to note the cultural context. The Samaritans were another group despised by the Jews. A good Jew would never speak to a Samaritan. Historians tell us there was great enmity between the Jews and the

Samaritans. But why did the Jews despise them so? They despised them because the Samaritans, who were descendents of Jacob, had intermarried outside the Jewish tradition. Since these Samaritans were no longer "pure Jews" they were considered heathen.

The Samaritans, and everything about them, was to be avoided. McGee points out, in his commentary on John 4, the disciples had gone into the city to buy food. They were buying Samaritan food. They might as well have bought pork chops for supper! Any food from these people would surely have been considered unclean to the self-respecting Jew.[11] Now don't miss this. Jesus not only allowed the disciples to buy meat in a Samaritan city. He also engaged a Samaritan woman in extended conversation. Jesus took the direct route to Cana through Samaria so he could meet with this woman. There were at least two alternate routes he could have taken. Instead, he went through Samaria, stopped at Jacob's well during the middle of the day, and spoke at length with this Samaritan woman.

So what did Jesus say to her? He said, "Will you give me a drink?"[12] The woman seemed immediately to know the significance of Jesus speaking to her in a civil way. She did not know exactly how to respond to his request, but she knew the significance of this Jewish man addressing her at this public place. She was at least curious why a Jewish man would ask her to serve him a drink when they both knew that Jews and Samaritans should have nothing to do with one another.

Through an extended exchange, this Samaritan woman discovered Jesus was—not just a Jewish man, but he was The Christ, the Messiah! She also discovered her real need for spiritual satisfaction which superseded her need for water of the well where they stood. In fact, the Bible says the woman left her waterpot, and went her way into the city. Wow! Hopefully, you can see how Jesus went literally out of his way to invest in building a cross-cultural faith experience.

Now maybe you are thinking, well those are isolated individual circumstances not really designed to extend Christ's ministry cross-culturally. Let me connect the story of Levi's call to ministry and the encounter with the Samaritan woman at the well. There is an interesting, common element in both these stories. After these two cultural "outcasts" met with the Lord, they were immediately changed. Today, we would say they were "on fire for Christ." In John chapter 4, the Samaritan woman went into the city and told all the men about Jesus and they came to see him for themselves. In verse 39, it is noted, "Many of the Samaritans of that town believed in him because of the woman's testimony." Jesus directly ministered cross-culturally to this woman and now, by extension, a previously excluded group of people was included in the family of God.

When Levi decided to follow Jesus, he went home and threw a big dinner party. He invited his fellow outcasts, the other tax collectors. He also invited Jesus. It is probably safe to assume some of them also believed in Jesus that day. Jesus Christ was direct and intentional about enabling cross-cultural worship. That is, he went out of his way to cross significant cultural barriers and to invite the excluded into belief in him.

Jesus also commanded us to do the same. I know what you're thinking. Where did Jesus command me to go out of my way to cross cultural barriers, and when did Jesus command me to invite the excluded into belief in Him? Well, I'm glad you wondered. This is clearly the point of Jesus' directive to all Christians as expressed in Acts chapter one and in Matthew chapter twenty eight. You may know these passages as "the great commission."

In Acts 1:8, Luke quotes Jesus as saying, "But ye shall receive power, after that the Holy Ghost is come upon you: and ye shall be witnesses unto me both in Jerusalem, and in all Judea, and in Samaria, and unto the uttermost part of the earth." This is the continuing commission Jesus first gave to the apostles, and through the scripture he has given to every Christian of every generation since that time. This continuing commission is pertinent to us even today.

Now what is this commission all about? The great commission is the express, timely instruction of Jesus for what the apostles were to do once he was removed from their physical presence. In Acts chapter one, we see the account of the Lord's ascension into heaven to sit at the right hand of God the Father. The context for Acts 1:8 is this:

Jesus had called together his eleven apostles. This takes place after Judas Iscariot had betrayed Christ, after the Lord's crucifixion, and after his resurrection from the dead. Jesus called the apostles together for final instructions. In Acts 1:4, Jesus told them to, "Wait for the promise of the Father." They were to wait in Jerusalem and the promise was they would be baptized with the Holy Spirit.

As they dialogued, just prior to the ascension, Jesus instructed the apostles regarding what they were to do "after" the Holy Spirit came upon them. And what were they to do? The Lord Jesus said, "Ye shall be witnesses unto me." In other words the apostles were to tell others about Jesus. They were to tell people who he was and what he did. This begs a few obvious questions or points for clarification. Who should be witnessing to whom and for how long? To answer these points, we need to bring another passage of scripture to the table.

As you may know, the great commission is also recorded by the apostle Matthew in his gospel account. Matthew quotes the Lord Jesus as saying, "Go ye therefore, and teach all nations, baptizing them in the name of the Father, and of the Son, and of the Holy Ghost: Teaching them to observe all things whatsoever I have commanded you: and lo, I am with you always, even unto the end of the world."

When we combine the language of Acts 1:8 with Matthew 28:19-20, we are able to more fully address the question of who should be witnessing to whom and for how long. So who should be witnessing or telling? Obviously the apostles, whom Jesus was addressing directly, were part of the expected group of witnesses. But were they to be the only witnesses? I think not because it would not be practical for them to carry out the mission alone. Jesus' commission was to be taken to the widest possible group. Jesus said take the message to, "The uttermost part of the earth." Jesus instructed that this message must be taught to, "All nations." Jesus knew that in order to fulfill this commission, the apostles would have to tell others, who would tell others, who would tell others. He knew this process of telling others would have to persist until one day someone would tell you and someone else would tell me, and you and I would hear of

Jesus and follow him. So this message, this testimony about Jesus, was to be told by every Christian in each succeeding generation. That means you are supposed to bear witness about Jesus too.

You, according to these verses, are supposed to tell the good news of Jesus Christ to all nations in every corner of the earth. You, according to Matthew 28, are supposed to spread this good news until the end of the earth. That is, until Jesus returns and establishes a new heaven and earth. Bottom line, you and every other Christian is commanded, indeed commissioned, by Jesus Christ to tell every non-Christian the message of who Jesus is and what he has done. Is that clear?

How, then, does this connect to the issue of cross-cultural worship? The insight is found in Jesus' description of the target audience. He says in the book of Matthew, the message must go to all nations. However, the route to all nations is clarified in Acts. Essentially Jesus says we are to take the message to all nations by beginning in Jerusalem, expanding to all of Judea, and Samaria, and ultimately to every part of the earth. So where do you think the church would encounter the cross-cultural challenge? We learn from the scriptures, that the cross-cultural challenge was seen and met at each stage of the early expansion of the gospel.

In Jerusalem, on the day of Pentecost, the Holy Spirit came upon the disciples as promised by Jesus before his ascension. When the Holy Spirit showed up, it was an amazing scene. According to Acts 2:5, there was a phenomenal diversity of people groups present in Jerusalem including Jews and devout men out of "every nation under heaven." The Bible says a multitude came together and they were confounded because "every man heard them speak in his own language." That multitude included a phenomenal diversity of ethnic, lingual and even religious backgrounds. These included Parthians, Medes, Elamites, Mesopotamians, those of Judea, Cappadocia, Pontus and Asia, Phrygians, Pamphylians, Libyans, Cyrenians, Arabians and those from Crete. Not only that, there were strangers of Rome, Jews and proselytes.[13] Among the Romans were proselytes—those who were converted to Judaism—so even the religious backgrounds of the people were varied. Obviously, the apostles encountered great cross-cultural diversity from the very beginning in Jerusalem. The Bible does not give any indication the apostles segregated all these people groups into little churches based upon ethnic or racial affinities.

In the verses following Acts 2:14, Peter stands and addresses this great multitude. He preached a message of unity in Jesus Christ. In verse 38, Peter invites the audience to, "Repent, and be baptized every one of you in the name of Jesus Christ for the remission of sins, and ye shall receive the gift of the Holy Spirit." Now wait a minute! Was Peter suggesting that all these non-Jews should receive the same Holy Spirit as the Jews who were among the crowd? Absolutely! We know this because Peter continued by saying, "For the promise is unto you, and to your children, and to all that are afar off, even as many as the Lord our God shall call." In verse 41, we see that all who received the Lord through Peter's message were baptized, and three thousand new people came into the family of God. So what do we learn from this? We learn the great commission was immediately effectuated across cultural barriers.

So, once the church began its expansion beyond Jerusalem, did it continue to address the issue of cross-cultural worship? Without a doubt the early Christian church did continue facing and embracing this challenge. According to Jesus' expansion plan, the church was to go from Jerusalem and the region of Judea into Samaria. As mentioned before, there would have been huge cross-cultural barriers seen in witnessing to the Samaritans. The Samaritans were a people formed through intermarriage of Jews with other people groups. The Samaritans no longer followed the strict Jewish traditions so there developed great hatred and enmity between the two groups. This formed a formidable cross-cultural barrier. Of note, Jesus had already modeled the "direct" approach he intended for the apostles and other disciples to take among the Samaritans.

As previously discussed, Jesus encountered the Samaritan woman at Jacob's well and changed her life. Jesus also used a Samaritan as the hero in his famous parable of one who helped another person who was in great need. This parable is often called "the parable of the Good Samaritan." In this parable or story, Jesus tells of a traveler who had sustained great injury and was left beside the road in great pain and suffering. The story is found in Luke chapter 10 when Jesus responds to a line of questions posed by a lawyer.

The lawyer asks, "What shall I do to inherit eternal life?" Jesus engages him in a very instructive dialogue about loving the Lord and loving others. Finally, the lawyer, trying to justify himself, asks Jesus, "Who is my neighbor?" Jesus responds with the parable of the Good Samaritan, explaining how a certain man traveling from Jerusalem down to Jericho was robbed by thieves, stripped of his clothing, beaten and left for dead. Several people passed the wounded man but none lifted a finger to help him. Finally, a Samaritan came and "had compassion on him." Jesus told of how this Samaritan man took excellent care of the wounded man by getting him help for his wounds and food and shelter for his recovery.

So what was Jesus teaching? He was teaching many profound truths in this story. By making the Samaritan the hero of the story, he was challenging the cross-cultural barrier that existed between his Jewish followers and this group of outcasts. When Jesus told this story, I'm sure it jolted his Jewish hearers. The lawyer who initiated the dialogue was probably stunned. In Luke 10:36, when Jesus completes the story, he asks of the lawyer, "Which of these three . . . was 'neighbor' to him that fell among thieves?" The lawyer replied, "He that showed mercy on him." In other words, the Good Samaritan was more of a neighbor to the injured man than his Jewish brethren. By admitting this, the lawyer (who was expert in the Jewish law and tradition) opened the possibilities for greater appreciation of non-Jews. In Jesus' story, the help was given "cross-culturally." Then, in verse 37, Jesus says to the lawyer, "Go and do thou likewise" clearly implying the lawyer should be a neighbor to those of other cultural backgrounds.

Now do you want to see something really special? Sure you do. To see it you must remember, this parable is given by Jesus in the context of an expert in Jewish law asking "Who is my neighbor?" You see Jesus was teaching this lawyer to re-think his notion of the neighborhood, even his notion of brotherhood. Jesus was teaching him that ethnic and racial affinity is not the determinant of brotherly love. He was teaching there is honor in extending oneself across traditionally taboo barriers of race and class and investing in the physical (and spiritual) development of others. We see in this example, Jesus fully intended for the outcast to be brought into the family of God. He told the lawyer to follow this example in his own behavior, and by extension, Jesus tells us to do the same today. Now isn't that special?

It is obvious that once the church would get beyond Samaria, it would encounter great ethnic and religious barriers. However, Jesus had instructed that among all these people groups, that is, those from among every nation, must be made disciples. So if Jesus really intended for all nations to receive the gospel message, then how did we ever get the notion we were somehow exempt from working across barriers to execute the great commission? What is so special about your ethnic group, or my racial group, or some other guy's language group that any of us should be released from the same cross-cultural challenge so obviously put to the apostles and to the early church? Do you have a good answer for this in light of Christ's clear directive, his personal example or the full counsel of the New Testament? If so, please write to me and explain it, because I honestly cannot understand why some folks in the CHURCH work so hard to preserve homogeneity "in the church."

Are you still tracking with me? Good! Hopefully, you now see Jesus clearly expected Christians to work across cultural and other barriers to build up the family of God. We will discuss other examples later in this book. We should now make the point that the early church took to heart Jesus' challenge toward cross-cultural worship. I am not saying it was always easy. I'm not even claiming there was no confusion within the church on this matter. However, I am thoroughly convinced by the evidence of the New Testament that the early church leaders built cross-cultural congregations by intentional effort and sought to perpetuate this tendency throughout the New Testament era. Let me give you a few examples.

The most obvious example of cross-cultural intent is seen in the ministry of the apostle Paul. His entire ministry would eventually focus upon the conversion of Gentiles to faith in Jesus Christ. His influence in this regard is readily seen in any serious study of the New Testament. In Acts 9 we learn of the "special" ministry the Lord called Paul to carry out. To grasp the special nature of his ministry calling, we have to go back to when Paul was called Saul.

Saul was a zealous leader among the Jewish religious establishment who saw the ministry of Jesus and His followers as a blasphemous and misguided group of rebels. In fact, Saul was notorious for his aggressive persecution of Christians. He saw it as his personal mission to stamp out this fledgling Christian sect and he used all his well-honed powers of persuasion and his well-earned influence as a Pharisee to accomplish that task. One could argue Saul was "over the top" in his determination to eradicate Christians. In Acts 7, Saul is shown standing by as a willing witness to the stoning death of Stephen, a young, enthusiastic Christian man. In Acts 8:1 the Bible notes, "At that time there was a great persecution against the church which was at Jerusalem; and they were all scattered abroad throughout the regions of Judea and Samaria, except the apostles." Then in verse 3 we read, "As for Saul, he made havoc of the church, entering into every house, and haling men and women committed them to prison." So Saul was, according to the Bible, an influential, action-oriented Pharisee who made it his daily priority to heap destruction upon the Christians he encountered. He stripped many of these Christians of their liberty and some of their very lives.

With this insight it is perhaps easier to see the special nature of his call to ministry. In Acts 9, the story is told of Saul's conversion experience and his call to ministry. It is noted, here, that Saul went to the high priest, threatening slaughter against the Christians. He asked the high priest for letters supporting his journey to Damascus. These letters would authorize Saul to speak in the synagogues along the way and empower him to seize and bind any Christian men and women he might encounter. Armed with the consent of the high priest, Saul departed for Damascus intending to capture these Christians and bring them back to imprisonment in Jerusalem. He had an agenda!

Saul did not know this was to be his last trip to round up and persecute Christians. He had no clue his life was about to be radically changed for the better. So what happened? Well, Saul, on his way to Damascus, was met by the resurrected Lord Jesus Christ! The Lord engaged Saul in a dialogue. At the end of their discussion, Saul had lost his sight and the Lord had instructed him to go into the city of Damascus. For three days Saul could not see, and he took no food or drink. During this time, the Lord also appeared to Ananias, a Christian disciple living in Damascus. Jesus then instructed Ananias where to meet Saul and what to say to him. But when Ananias heard the name Saul he was greatly put off by it. Ananias checked to see if Jesus knew who this Saul guy really was and what he was doing to the church. It is during this discussion, and in this amazing context, that Jesus says to Ananias of Saul, "He is a chosen vessel unto me, to bear my name before the Gentiles."

Wow! Given his background, no one could believe the Lord would call such a man to the ministry of the gospel. Ananias certainly could not believe it. Neither did the other Damascan Jews believe it when they heard Saul preach about Jesus in the synagogues.[14] Afterward, when Saul went to Jerusalem he had no Christian prisoners. Not only this, but he sought to "get connected" with the Christians at Jerusalem. When he came to the Christian disciples, they not only disbelieved he was a Christian, but they were afraid of him.[15] Again, given Saul's background, this is more than understandable. Eventually, Barnabas convinced the brethren that Saul was a legitimate Christian. When I think of the life Saul led prior to his Christian conversion, and his unique calling by the resurrected Jesus Christ, I find it absolutely amazing.

But even more amazing, is the realization of what Saul was called to do. In Acts 22, we find the account of Paul's reflection upon his own conversion experience. He then reflects upon his return to Jerusalem. While he was praying in the temple at Jerusalem, he saw a vision of the Lord.[16] The Lord warned Paul of the trouble he would face in Jerusalem and in Acts 22:21, Jesus gives Paul his ministry assignment—a ministry to the Gentiles. So let me recap what has happened. This guy Saul, a devout and over-zealous Jewish leader meets Jesus on a road trip to Damascus. Jesus humbles Saul to a point of blindness and a three-day fast. Then Jesus calls this same Saul (who after his conversion was called Paul) to preach the gospel message. Not only that, but Jesus gives Paul a specific ministry to the Gentiles. I probably don't need to tell you how unlikely it was that Paul would be a Christian at all. Surely, you can now see how amazing it is that Paul would actually be called to Christian ministry. But could you, in your wildest moment of imagination, ever think this same Paul would be given perhaps the most critical role in perhaps the greatest and most enduring challenge facing the church—the ministry of cross-cultural worship?

Paul would say of his ministry calling, "The Gentiles should be fellow heirs, and of the same body, and partakers of his promise in Christ by the gospel. Whereof I was made a minister, according to the gift of the grace of God given unto me by the effectual working of his power. Unto me, who am less than the least of all saints, is this grace given, that I should preach among the Gentiles the unsearchable riches of Christ."[17] It is clear to me the apostle Paul was given the clear and compelling mandate to operate across cultures to build up this Christian movement he once so aggressively destroyed. Later, we will examine some of the evidence of how Paul built up many Christian congregations. Again, any serious study of Paul's ministry will reveal his intent to build Christian environments wholly conducive to cross-cultural worship.

For another proof of how leadership in the early church grasped and executed Christ's intent toward cross-cultural worship, we should look briefly at the account of Peter's firm conviction on this point. Peter's experience is also very important in making the case for cross-cultural worship. In Acts 10, the apostle Peter, also known as Simon Peter, had his horizon expanded. The story is told of how Simon Peter was staying in Joppa at the home of Simon the tanner. One day, at lunch time, Peter went up on the rooftop to pray. He was also very hungry, but while his food was being prepared Peter fell into a trance. What happened next changed his outlook on the ministry.

Peter saw a vision of heaven opening up, and he saw something like a sheet tied together at the four corners descending upon the earth. Inside this massive sheet he saw four-footed beasts, wild beasts, creeping things and birds. Then, he heard a voice saying, "Rise, Peter, kill and eat." Peter, in his vision, rejected this offer to eat on the basis that he had "never" eaten any impure or unclean foods.[18] Again, he heard the voice saying, "Do not call anything impure that God has made clean."[19] The voice repeated these words three times and the memory was, no doubt, forever etched in Peter's mind.

Initially, Peter did not understand the vision and he continued pondering its meaning. On the next day, Peter traveled from Joppa to Caesarea to visit with Cornelius the centurion. Amazingly, Cornelius had also had a vision in which he was instructed to send to Joppa for Peter. You see, the Lord had given these two men a vision and arranged for them to meet. This is a great example of what you might call a "divine appointment." By the time Peter arrived at Cornelius' house, a crowd had gathered. Now I want you to see something in this meeting setting: Peter was a Jew and Cornelius was a Gentile. So the Lord had orchestrated a cross-cultural meeting to bring a powerful revelation into the life of Peter. Now hold that thought.

Peter and Cornelius talked and they entered Cornelius' home. When Peter saw the crowd, he began to preach using insight he had garnered from the vision of the Lord. Now wait a minute. Do you see what just happened? The Lord had not only orchestrated a cross-cultural meeting between two men, but He had arranged a cross-cultural worship experience for the two men and a crowd of people from both Jewish and Gentile backgrounds. Now it is in this context Peter begins to preach. The significance of the cross-cultural audience was not lost on Peter for he started by saying to the crowd, "You are well aware that it is against our law for a Jew to associate with a Gentile or visit him. But God has shown me that I should not call any man impure or unclean."[20] So Peter asks why he has been asked to come to this place. Cornelius answers by recounting the vision he had received which prompted him to send for Peter. Afterward, Cornelius says, "Now we are all here in the presence of God to listen to everything the Lord has commanded you to tell us." It was in this moment the light bulb of understanding was turned on in Peter's mind. In this moment, it seems, Peter grasped the meaning of the vision God had given to him.

Speaking from the heart, Peter says, "I now realize how true it is that God does not show favoritism but accepts men from every nation who fear him and do what is right." He then told them about Jesus—how the Lord ministered to many throughout that region. He told them how Jesus was crucified, and how God raised him from the dead to be seen of many witnesses. He told them how Jesus had commanded them to preach to the people. And then Peter told the crowd, "Everyone who believes in him receives forgiveness of sins through his name." And guess what happened—while Peter was still preaching—the Holy Spirit came upon all who heard the message.

The Bible says the circumcised believers who had come with Peter were astonished to see the Holy Spirit come upon the Gentiles. Clearly, they too had their horizons expanded on that day. Then Peter, not wanting to waste the moment, said, "Can anyone keep these people from being baptized with water as they have received the Holy Spirit just as we have." So they were baptized in the name of Jesus Christ.

After a few days, Peter went to Jerusalem and shared all these things with the believers there. Initially some were angered to hear Peter had gone into the house of a Gentile. But as Peter explained further it became clear the Lord was in this experience. He told how the Spirit had come upon the uncircumcised just as it had come upon him and his fellow Jewish converts. Peter went on to say, "Then I remembered what the Lord had said: 'John baptized with water, but you will be baptized with the Holy Spirit.' So if God gave them (Gentiles) the same gift (the Holy Spirit) as he gave us (Jews) who believed in the Lord Jesus Christ, who was I to think that I could oppose God?"

In Acts 11:18, we learn that when the Jerusalem church heard what Peter said, they had no further objections and praised God saying, "So then, God has granted even the Gentiles repentance unto life." In other words, with the unanimous consent of the Jerusalem church, the headquarter congregation, the gospel was now to go forward directly to the Gentiles. This changed the ministry of Peter and the resolve of the church in a decisively cross-cultural direction.

Did you catch Peter's rhetorical question at the end of his case before the Jerusalem church? He asked, ". . . Who was I to think I could oppose God?" You may recall, at the beginning of this book, I asked you the same question. Like Peter, I still wonder who we think we are to oppose God's plan for his church. I am thoroughly convinced anyone in the Christian community who is still trying to hold on to a homogeneous worship experience—a homogeneous church—is on the wrong side of the obvious implication of Peter's rhetorical question. Such a person must somehow see themselves as exempt from the direction so clearly established in the early church.

So let me bring all this back together. We have been discussing the biblical evidence that the early church understood and acted upon the biblical mandate for cross-cultural worship. We have seen how the two primary leaders of the early church, the apostles Peter and Paul, clearly and unequivocally concluded that the Christian ministry was to be cross-cultural. I think the case for cross-cultural worship is clearly made in the New Testament. I think, by now, you may be convinced of the case for cross-cultural worship. However, I also know there will be some who say, I grant you Peter and Paul had visions that shaped their ministries for cross-cultural emphasis, but were the new churches formed actually cross-cultural in composition? They would argue, yes, we agree the church was now to spread across racial and ethnic barriers. But where in the Bible do we see the multi-ethnic, multi-racial model presented as an example to follow?

Whilst you and I are already on the boat, we mustn't run off and leave others who have this nagging reservation. So where is the "model church" which presents the case for cross-cultural worship? I believe that model is seen in the church at Antioch. This important church had become a key outpost, called by some the new headquarters of the rapidly expanding Christian Church.

In the church at Antioch, we observe a critical point in the composition of the leadership team. The team included Barnabas; Simeon called Niger; Lucius of Cyrene; Manaen and Saul. Keep in mind, here, the early church was spreading outward from Jerusalem in keeping with the command of Christ to be witnesses in Jerusalem, Judea and Samaria, and to the ends of the earth.[21] When the church reached Antioch, we see a very important development. Washington and Kehrein, in their book *Breaking Down Walls*, made the observation this Antioch church had a cross-cultural leadership team. In their book, they referred to this finding as "the principle of shared leadership." When these two men started their joint ministry in Chicago, they implemented the Antioch model with much-heralded success. Their idea was in order to develop and sustain a diverse congregation it is important to begin with shared or culturally diverse leadership.

The Antioch leadership team, as recorded in Acts 13, was cross-cultural with widely variant personal backgrounds. There was Lucius, from Cyrene on the north coast of Africa; Simeon who we seem to know little about; Manaen who lived among the Roman elite and was reared with Herod the Tetrarch; Barnabas, the Cypriot Jew of the tribe of Levi; and of course, Saul or Paul who came from the elite, Pharisaical leadership of the Jewish establishment. This leadership team was by no means ethnically homogeneous. No doubt, these men brought different perspectives and sensitivities to the church at Antioch and all subsequent ministry to which they were engaged. I don't know if you have had the opportunity, as I have, to be part of a diverse leadership team. It is amazing to see how the varying perspectives necessarily generate more possibilities which almost always seem to produce better ideas and solutions. When you have been part of a diverse and successful team, you tend neither to forget the experience nor to stray far from the lessons of such shared leadership.

I suppose, for these men, their time together in Antioch was full of possibilities. I suspect the varied backgrounds of these men helped to build and support a very integrated congregation at Antioch. When the time came for them to break company, I'm sure they would have carried the lessons with them. Of course, this team did break up when Barnabas and Paul were called to new work. The two men ministered together in Seleucia, in Cyprus, in Perga and Pamphylia. Paul continued on this missionary journey and other journeys also recorded in the scriptures. However, from this experience in Antioch until the time of his death, I find no evidence in the New Testament where Paul established a homogeneous church. What reason is there for us to believe the Antioch model of shared leadership and integrated congregations is not the model most consistently employed in all the subsequent church plants discussed in the chronicle of Paul's journeys? I think the early church got it! It saddens me to see how, in our day, we either don't get it or have gotten it and decided we don't want it! Again I ask you, who are we to think we should oppose God?

The New Testament is replete with examples of integrated congregations, attendant with all the challenges one would expect from cross-cultural interaction. In Paul's letters to the churches at Ephesus and Corinth, big cities of that era, we see how he speaks directly to some of the challenges of cross-cultural worship. We see how ethnic groups do sometimes create interpersonal strife. We see arguments over the ministration of the Lord's Supper; discord around the treatment of one group's widows by another group in the church; and disagreements over what could be worn or eaten among the brethren. However, in none of these matters do we see a recommendation from Paul's or Peter's letters suggesting the churches split into affinity groups or form homogeneous congregations elsewhere. Instead, the advice from these Pauline and Petrine letters is clearly for the churches to work across these barriers and to see the possibilities arising from working together. Because of these admonitions to stay and pray together, the Lord's Supper is less of a focus on "the meal" and more of a pure focus on the sacrifice of Jesus with a small wafer of bread and a thimbleful of wine. Because of their insistence that these churches stay and pray together, the widows were well cared for and the office of deacon was established.

Indeed cross-cultural worship is a good thing. It is supported in scripture by the direct and intentional example of Jesus Christ, and it is clear the early church leaders understood the imperative and acted toward this model in the establishment and perpetuation of the Christian churches. So we have seen a compelling biblical mandate for cross-cultural worship. For this reason, we must take our efforts back to the basics. We must do all in our power to return to the New

Testament style integration of the believers and eradicate all such racial and ethnic segregation in the faith. This we can do proactively. It should, however, be noted there is a practical argument to this issue.

The Empirical Facts

Maybe you accept the Biblical mandate for cross-cultural worship. I rejoice with you. Perhaps, though, you would say Witherspoon is right, but I still choose to continue pursuing a course of segregated worship. Well, in that case I hate to be the bearer of bad news, but the physical reality outside your church is also working very much against homogeneity. The empirical data does not bode well for the future of your ministry to a mono-ethnic, mono-racial, and likely aging congregation. Let me explain why.

There is a decisive and now even obvious trend toward urbanization. If you live in a big city anywhere in the world you will notice a few almost universal truths. Now by big city I mean the modern-day megalopolis, that is, cities with more than a million residents. In such cities one can easily see there is great physical diversity among the population. This has been driven to some degree by the increased opportunity to work and meet people in the big city versus the smaller towns.

Today, nearly half the world's population, or more than three billion people, live in cities! Ray Bakke, in his book *A Theology as Big as the City*, correctly predicted, "The spectacular growth of large cities would represent an awesome challenge to the church of Jesus Christ on all six continents. In 1900, 8 percent of the world's population lived in cities. By the year 2000, that number will be nearly 50 percent."[22]

Bakke was right, and according to 2005 global statistical data, 48.7 percent of all people live in the world's cities.[23] Dramatic consolidation is being seen in the largest of these cities. Over 22 percent of the world's population lives in about 400 megalopolises or urban areas with populations of 1 million or more residents, and there are 20 cities with more than 10 million residents.[24] So why is that important? Because concentration into large cities brings people into close proximity, and larger cities attract people of all types for the reasons already discussed. Now when people come together from different backgrounds they do indeed begin to open up more possibilities for working and connecting with each other.

It is a fact of demographic reality people will come together across racial, ethnic, and most other barriers. My observation from traveling to some of the largest cities in the world—cites such as Tokyo, Seoul, Mexico City, New York, Shanghai, Bombay, Delhi, Los Angeles, Jakarta, Cairo, Manila and others—is people seem to move very comfortably across race and ethnicity. They readily form cross-cultural associations and even cross-cultural and inter-ethnic intimate relationships. That's a good thing, right? Well here is the thing to think about in all this demographic reality: the rapid urbanization of the world's cities has brought with it the rapid expansion of new values, products and lifestyles. As we might expect from past experience, these newly developing values, products and lifestyles are often incompatible with the Christian ethic. The point is if the church undertook a conscious effort to develop biblical standards for how cities should address cross-cultural interaction, our approach might well differ from the world's approach. If the church fails, however, to address the new urban reality, the world's perspective will prevail. I don't know about you, but I cannot sit back and allow the worldly system or popular society to determine the values for cross-cultural interaction with no voice from the Christian community of born-again believers.

Just think for a moment about those worldly values, products and lifestyles. Popular society is now able to introduce and expand an idea much quicker than any time in history. The advent of mass communication vehicles and access to monstrously large repositories of interconnected data via the internet, have made it possible for one to get information instantaneously with very little effort. Of course television, radio and digital entertainment media, combined with the internet and the visual media of print and billboards and the like literally bombard the average city-dweller with millions of images and sound-bites every single day. As the world converges on the acceptable norms, mores and values of each population center, these can be quickly integrated into the thinking of the unsuspecting citizen.

The values, oh the values are dangerous. Already, we can see popular society values are clashing with Christian values. Already, we can see corporations developing and pushing popular products which fly in the face of the Judeo-Christian standards of basic right and wrong. My friends, on any given day you can undoubtedly observe lifestyle choices that contravene biblical teaching.

I am not suggesting we can or should stop society from developing these values, products and lifestyles. I am, however, saying if we do not address the values required for harmonious and cross-cultural interaction in the church, then many Christians and prospective Christians will be left to adopt the societal standard. This would be a tragic outcome. Unfortunately, this reality is already playing out in many Christian congregations.

So let's think about it for a moment. Billions of people now live in the world's big cities. Population densities are higher than any point in the past. This means people are living in closer and closer proximity to people who are different from themselves. In response to this demographic reality, federal and municipal governments are forced to adjust the rules of engagement for people to interact across previously impermeable barriers. For example, in places where it was once illegal or socially unacceptable to marry outside ones race, interracial unions are more common and accepted. This is an important leading indicator, because marriage is still the ultimate expression of one group's "acceptance" of another. More people are challenging the previously taboo beliefs about falling in love across racial and ethnic lines. Again, this is very evident in the big cities of the world. Not only that, but people seem less content to associate along narrowly defined parameters of race or class. Those who are well-traveled have gained exposure to people of other backgrounds. Some people, me included, find it almost unimaginable to only have one type of friend from one type of background.

Big cities, now touting greater diversity among their residents and more favorable conditions for cross-cultural interaction, are attracting even larger and more diverse populations. As big cities grow, especially if they grow due to an influx of productive laborers, they expand their capacity for future growth. This dynamic creates a virtuous cycle where big cities attract more people, grow their tax base, and invest to create the environment where more people want to come. The big just keep getting bigger.

Small and medium sized cities do the same thing, but on a smaller scale consistent with their resources. To compete with the bigger cities, some cities try to establish niches by designing unique and planned communities. Others build their appeal around features such as natural cites or entertainment centers. But fewer and fewer places are able to successfully grow and thrive on a platform of racial or ethnic separatism. Even exclusive locations find it difficult to exclude on the basis of race, and high prices are no longer sufficient to block entry of people with different backgrounds.

Employers, public and private, get in on the act because they too must create the environmental conditions which attract the best talent. As the demographics of urbanization would indicate, more and more of the top talent want to live in big cities which offer the amenities and environment they require. Companies therefore find themselves investing in the kinds of municipal features which help to attract such talent. This explains why companies invest in the local arts venues, sporting and entertainment, city-center development and other projects which make cities more attractive to prospective employees. It seems everyone is working to do their part in determining how society addresses the challenge of different people coming together to live and work.

But where is the church? Is there a role for the church to play in determining how people—especially Christians—should operate cross-culturally? I firmly believe the church has a role. Our failure to engage this topic will be a haunting legacy for Christianity and the overall cause of Christ. I think fewer professionals and young people will be interested in congregations which offer little or no diversity. These folks will grow weary living a double life. It will be difficult for people to live and work with people of all types of backgrounds and to find relevance in a homogeneous church setting. I know some churches, even large churches, are getting away with this duplicity today. However, I think those ministries have a poor future outlook. They may look vibrant and growing, but the reality of segregation is eating away like a cancer from inside. This cancer, though undetected is deadly. The prognosis for such a church is not good. It may even be fatal.

It saddens me deeply to be in a world-class city and to see the wonderful cross-cultural interaction of so many people and to know that come Sunday morning so many Christians will worship in segregated churches. For me it is a big "disconnect" for the church with reality. I'm writing to you so your eyes would be opened to the folly of this behavior. Unlike the explosive growth of cities, most churches are stagnant. The average church still plateaus at about 200 congregants. Why do you think this happens? It is not because the message lacks relevance! It is because the methods lack appeal. Too many of today's churches are insular. The balance between edifying the saints and evangelizing the lost is out of whack. Churches often spend more time catering to current parishioners and ignoring the physical and spiritual needs of the communities they serve. Somewhere along the way, Christians got the idea the faith was all about being comfortable and being catered to like we expect in a restaurant or a hotel. Christ never called us to be comfortable Christians unmoved by the needs of others. Jesus taught that we should be willing to suffer and that it is honorable to serve others.

You see, the more we resist the challenge of cross-cultural worship, the less we will truly engage the cities where most people live. Healthier churches create touch points in all corners of the community. Churches active in all areas of a community tend to have a composition representative of the touch points where they invest. If a church is homogeneous, especially in a modern city, it is because they have a ministry which does not "touch" all points in the community. The obvious question is why a church would choose not to touch a segment of its community. I can't answer that for all churches, but I believe segregated churches in cross-cultural cities are destined for extinction. Not only are they tending to create an environmental reality fewer people will tolerate, they are working against the end game of Jesus Christ and his church.

In a later chapter I will share my experiences in three very different churches. Some of my most important observations have come from watching and working in those fellowships. Some of those experiences have been hugely positive and have changed my life and my outlook on the possibilities for cross-cultural worship. I am anxious to share those stories and the principles gleaned from each example.

WHY WE DENY OR DELAY

To this point, we have discussed the case for why the church must move with intent toward cross-cultural worship. We have seen the biblical mandate and observed that Jesus spoke clearly to this challenge and the early church understood and acted upon the mandate. We have seen how demographics are changing the way people live and interact with one another. We have talked about the environment outside the church and how congregations should reflect communities.

Earlier, I promised to return to the matter of "excuses" and this next section addresses the point. There are so many excuses presented by church leaders for why they are not engaging the cross-cultural challenge that I could not list them all in this book. Even if I could articulate them all, it would be too depressing for anyone to read. My intent, here, is to share some of what I have heard and learned about why many churches seem to deny the importance of cross-cultural worship or delay its implementation. Scholarship requires I, at least, present the opposing view.

The Next Enduring Frontier

Over the years the church has developed working approaches to some of the largest challenges of the times. We have learned, at least to a certain extent, how to be "in" the world but not "of" the world. That is, we have learned to address many of the most enduring real-world challenges without giving up our Christian distinctiveness. The church has learned how to influence the authorities governing our communities without having direct control over those governments. The church has learned to find common ground, despite denominational rifts, to serve communities in times of great need (e.g., natural disaster relief, pandemic disease eradication). But we have not as yet adequately addressed the challenge of cross-cultural worship. Sadly, racial and ethnic divide still troubles our world and still exists in our churches.

Racial and ethnic reconciliation is the last enduring frontier left for the church to address and tackle. This area—racial reconciliation—has become a sticky wicket for many believers. Many have sought to avoid the matter by finding escape in homogeneous congregations. Of interest, many of these same Christians have adjusted to the changing demographics of the workplace. They have learned to work with a diverse employee population, yet they cannot see the merit of cross-cultural worship. This puzzles me so I have been asking pastors and congregants alike to explain it to me. When I ask such questions, I do not often get data-based or even Bible-based responses. What I get, more often than not, is an earful of excuses.

To explain these excuses and drive clarity of the issue, I want to focus this part of our discussion on the specific cross-cultural challenge of working across racial and ethnic lines of demarcation. I know some of you are saying, there he goes with the race thing. You're right. While I realize the cross-cultural challenge includes all types of barriers, I'm going specifically into the race thing. Now why would I do such a thing? I'm focusing our attention on race because I have observed that if one truly addresses the causes of racial segregation in the church, other barriers like age, class and gender can be more readily addressed. I have seen that race and ethnicity are among the most difficult.

These excuses for not addressing racial reconciliation tend to fall into two big themes. First, there is the large number of excuses rooted in the fear of reconciliation. Second, there is a set of excuses rooted in the fallacy of affinity. Let us now look at both these groups of excuses.

The Fear of Reconciliation

Many in the church are unwilling to engage the challenge of cross-cultural worship because they are smitten with a fear of reconciliation. What is reconciliation? For our purposes, reconciliation is a multi-level strategy to bring Christians together across race (and other barriers) into a state of symbiosis characterized by a high trust level, candid communication and shared leadership.

I know this is a bit of a comprehensive definition but it is important for us to be clear what we are talking about when discussing the topic of reconciliation. Experience has taught me the word reconciliation conjures up a variety of emotions in people. In an American context, when folks hear the phrase racial reconciliation, they think of slavery. Black folks think about their forefathers never receiving the promised "forty acres and a mule"; white folks think somebody is getting ready to ask them to apologize for societal ills they had no personal part in causing; and everybody else is thinking what does the African American's enslavement have to do with me? So why do I use such a term knowing it might be received in so many different ways?

It's simple, I use the term reconciliation (even racial reconciliation) because "reconciliation" is the precise term used in a "racial" context in scripture to describe the enduring challenge we are now discussing. I'll come to specific passages in a moment, but I bring up this topic and use these particular words, however inflammatory or perturbing, to elicit those very emotions I know some of you now feel. I want you a little uncomfortable right now. Being too comfortable on this topic, generally by avoiding it or making excuses, has gotten us in the mess we now find ourselves. I know it is uncomfortable to talk about slavery and painful discord in the body of Christ. But we must talk about it. Indeed, we must do something about it! The discomfort does not belie the need.

The need for racial reconciliation in the Christian Church has never been more evident, urgent or deadly. Although the early church developed principles and practices to enable reconciliation between the races, the modern church has slowly, but steadily, unlearned them. From the ancient past to the modern and post-modern present we have developed and perpetuated models of individualism leading to racial division and inter-racial strife in the church. Smitten by the evil bite of slavery, American Christians were scarred early on in the development of our nation. Our forefathers, many of whom were Christians, fell victim to false beliefs of racial superiority, and perpetuated the pattern of racial animosity already adopted in the larger society. The ugly pattern of animosity led directly to the formation of strategies for segregation, and those strategies crept into the church and eventually became part of the fabric of Christian life in the 18th century churches of the fledgling, upstart nation now known as The United States of America.

Let's get real for a moment. To preserve the financial interests afforded by the slavery and indentured servant system found in early American history, it was important to maintain the economic and social separation of the races. Though there is no basis for it in New Testament theology, it was also preached in many pulpits, and taught in slave-holding homes that we should maintain a spiritual segregation as well.[25] The devastating impact of these decisions has been visited upon the sons and daughters of the American Christian community even to the third, fourth and fifth generation.

America is not alone. Churches in Europe and Asia have likewise suffered the ill-fortune of the philosophy of segregation. After all, America is a young nation and it did not invent the idea of slavery, nor did the American church invent the idea of segregation it would eventually hold so dear. Racial and ethnic division has impacted the churches on all the inhabited continents, including Africa. Division and segregation have become the rule and not the exception. When I have attended and preached in churches across the world, I have seen the sad reality of segregation and the missed opportunity to witness effectively in culturally diverse settings.

Christians have erected barrier upon barrier to preserve their traditions and their racial and ethnic heritage. Though never intended by Christ, these barriers of race and ethnicity form unnecessary and almost impermeable lines of demarcation. These lines divide our churches and scream to the world Christians are no different than anyone else when it comes to the ability to truly love our neighbors without respect to skin color or place of origin. Well guess what? The world is now changing in its attitude toward racial and ethnic harmony, and the church is still stuck in the mud of ethnic disunity and racial self-preservation. We are sowing, among ourselves, the very seeds of segregation. The struggle for individual identity has found a willing cohort in the philosophy of affinity. I'll address this point more fully later, but the tragedy is for too many Christians individual identity has taken precedence over the common identity we have in Christ Jesus. I remind you, if you are a Christian, you must render unto Caesar that which is his. However, I also say to you, as a Christian, that your true and enduring citizenship is in heaven. You may live in Rome, but the Bible does not actually implore us to do as the Romans do. Whilst it may be important to be a Roman, a Chinese, an American, an Australian, a Nigerian, a Canadian, a Lithuanian, or even an Iranian, it is far more important to be a Christian. The one is temporal, the other is eternal.

I said I would share a scriptural basis for racial reconciliation. The New Testament is replete with support for a concerted and intentional effort toward racial reconciliation within the body of Christ. Christ, himself, gave priority to this directive in response to a Pharisee who asked, "Master, which is the greatest commandment in the law?" The Lord answered, "Love the Lord your God with all your heart and with all your soul and with all your mind."[26] In this response, Jesus addresses the first-order need of reconciliation: our need to be reconciled to God. This was the reason Christ came. He came so you and I could hear and receive the message of salvation, and thereby be reconciled to God who is the Father of all creation. Jesus, however, continued in his response to the Pharisee. He said, "Love your neighbor as yourself." Here, Jesus addresses the second-order need of reconciliation: that we are reconciled to one another. Now don't miss this next point. Jesus then said to the Pharisee, "All the law and the prophets hang on these two commandments." Wow! Could it really be that simple?

Do you see what just happened? Jesus just told a Pharisee, an expert in the Old Testament scripture, the most important commandment in all of the Old Testament scripture is to love God and love your neighbor. He essentially told this Pharisee the most important commandment is for us to execute the "ministry of reconciliation." Let me explain why I am saying this. When Jesus says love your "neighbor" as yourself, he was giving these remarks a decidedly cross-cultural context. Remember the parable of the Good Samaritan we discussed earlier? Let us re-examine the key questions leading up to the parable being spoken. Recall, the Pharisee first asked, "What must I do to inherit eternal life?" After Jesus quoted Deuteronomy 6:5, the Pharisee asked, "Who is my neighbor?" Jesus then replied with the parable of the Good Samaritan. But here is the kicker. When the Lord had told the Pharisee of the priest, the Levite and the Samaritan who each saw the injured man on the roadside, he ended with the key question designed for the Pharisee to self-discover the high and noble truth and the moral of the story. What was the Lord's concluding question—that all-important "food for thought" question? Jesus asked the Pharisee, "Which of these three do you think was a "neighbor" to the man who fell into the hands of robbers?"

The answer to the parable is "The Samaritan" was more of a neighbor. The Pharisee gave the correct answer. His neighbor was the one who is most unlike him—for a Pharisee, the Samaritan was a polar opposite. So in our passage in Matthew 22, as in the Good Samaritan parable of Luke 10, Jesus is making the point of reconciliation a decidedly cross-cultural, indeed a cross-racial one.

Now that you are nibbling on the bait, let me set this hook for you. Consider Second Corinthians chapter 5, beginning in verse 17. Here is where the scripture uses the word reconciliation. Here is where the rubber starts to hit the road. Up to this point, you may have been telling yourself it was okay to push this work of reconciliation onto someone else's plate. You may have convinced yourself that you were already dealing with a full plate of ministry, and simply had no room for the ministry of reconciliation. To be blunt, you may have felt you could somehow shirk this responsibility. Well I'm here to tell you there is no such option available to you. Let me tell you why.

In Second Corinthians, the Apostle Paul presents, in no uncertain terms, how "all" believers are to engage the ministry of reconciliation. In chapter 5, beginning with verse 14, Paul lays this imperative before us. Here is Paul's logic track. If Christ died for "all" then "all" were destined to die. But if some of us "live" then we should live for Christ and not for ourselves (it seems the least we could do). Then, in verse 16, Paul said something really special when he penned, "So from now on we regard no man from a worldly point of view. Though we once regarded Christ in this way, we do so no longer." I have been reflecting on this statement. I believe Paul is teaching we must look at all people differently. We must no longer see them from a worldly or physical perspective. Well, from what perspective, then, are we now to see people? We are to stop seeing people as temporal beings who simply live and die and cease to exist. We must now see "all" people as spiritual beings with an eternal destiny.

In verse 17, Paul continues by bringing it home to us as Christians. He says, "If anyone is in Christ", that is, if anyone is a Christian, "He is a new creation." He says God, in making us a new creation, has done two things. First, he has "reconciled" us to himself through Christ. There is that word again. The Greek word, *katallasso*, is here translated reconcile; and is used of the divine work of redemption insofar as God himself, by taking upon himself our sin and becoming an atonement, establishes that relationship of peace with mankind which the demands of his justice have previously prevented.[27] We should note here, God is the subject and man is the object, so God does the reconciling. So what is the second thing God has done with "all" Christians? He has given us the "ministry of reconciliation." Be honest, did you know before now that every single Christian has been given, by God himself, the ministry of reconciliation? Well if you didn't know, now you know that you have received the ministry of reconciliation, that is, if you are a Christian. Paul goes on to point out, in verse 19, God has given us the message of reconciliation. This indicates that the point of our message to the world—the point of the gospel—is to share God's plan of reconciliation through Jesus Christ.

Let me summarize the logic track so we are on the same page: every Christian is a new creation of God's and each of us has been reconciled to God. This means God has made his peace with us. God has also given us the ministry and the message of reconciliation, and we are to be his ambassadors (verse 20) who boldly go and tell everyone they too should be reconciled to God. This is the logic used by the Apostle Paul, and it binds every Christian to the work of reconciliation.

We get another piece of the reconciliation puzzle in Paul's letter to the church at Ephesus. This piece fits perfectly with the Second Corinthians passage. In Ephesians 2, speaking of Jesus Christ, Paul says, "For he is our peace, who has made both one, and has broken down the middle wall of partition between us; having abolished in his flesh the enmity (or hatred), even the law of commandments contained in ordinances; for to make in himself of twain one new man, so making peace; and that he might reconcile both unto God in one body by the cross, having slain the enmity thereby."

In this passage, Paul teaches us that Jesus brought about that peace which Second Corinthians described as coming when each of us is reconciled to God. In fact, Jesus is that peace. Such peace was achieved when Jesus died on the cross for us. The reference, in Ephesians, to breaking down the middle wall, is a reminder of how the curtain (middle wall) in the temple was torn in two when Christ was crucified. This wall or curtain was the dividing line in the temple. Beyond this point, as we discussed, no Gentile could pass without literally taking a mortal risk to do so. This physical barrier between Jew and Gentile was destroyed, and along with it went the enmity (or at least the reason for such enmity). So how did Christ destroy the enmity between the Jews and Gentiles? According to Ephesians chapter 2, verse 16, Jesus destroyed this hatred by reconciling both unto God in one body by the cross. He destroyed the enmity between Jew and Gentile by making of the two one new man.

Did you notice that Jesus reconciled both Jew and Gentile to God? Well if you caught that, then surely you saw the fact he reconciled them into "one body" by the cross. By this we see Jesus brought both Jews and Gentiles together across races into one body of believers. Clearly, this indicates the intent of Christ to establish a cross-cultural church comprised of both Jews and Gentiles who have been transformed from the lower-order identities of Jews or Gentiles into the higher-order identity of Christians.

In the face of such biblical evidence one must wonder why so many Christian leaders still choose to avoid the challenge of racial reconciliation? Jesus did not avoid the challenge. Paul did not avoid the challenge. Why do church leaders, who are generally well versed in the teachings of Christ and often deeply familiar with the New Testament, take a passive position on integration in the church? I want to focus here upon the attitudes of our church leaders because I believe today's lack of cross-cultural worship is first of all a leadership issue. Christians are looking to their leadership for proper interpretation of scripture and definition of the practical standards for everyday living flowing from that interpretation. For this reason, it is imperative that Christian leaders get on the right side of this discussion—and preferably get there first.

Earlier, I said some actually have a fear of racial reconciliation, and I believe this is often the case. Sadly, this is the case among both the clergy and the laity. But what could they possibly have to fear? I have observed two big reasons why Christians often fear racial reconciliation: they either fear losing what they do have or they fear gaining what they don't have. With both these fears, there is a common denominator and it is the fear of the unknown.

So what do our Christian leaders fear losing? Based upon scores of personal interviews and thousands of surveys I have administered, I believe many Christian leaders fear losing the comfort which comes from knowing a thing inside and out. When it comes to leading a congregation almost entirely comprised of people from their same race, many of these leaders expect there will be few surprises. They know if you will, what to expect and the way things should work. In their minds, the way things work is through homogeneous congregational models. Christian leaders fear losing that homogeneity. They fear losing the comfort zone of familiarity. I guess this is to be expected since so many Christian leaders—like most Christians—have grown up in homogeneous church environments. A part of them says, "It was good enough for my mother, its good enough for me." Our Christian leaders have been trained in bible colleges and seminaries where they were taught homogeneous models for church development and church growth. Never mind the fact that such conventional models no longer work as well. Most Christian churches are stagnant to declining in size and scope. Congregations are becoming more splintered and less effective. Despite the negative growth in most churches around the world, many church leaders are still clinging to these ineffective models. The fear of losing this familiar model scares some of our leaders to no end. These same leaders then take pastorates in homogeneous churches and further perpetuate a pattern of homogeneity. They associate almost entirely with pastors and leaders from their same race. They gravitate to members who are most like them, and for many the thought of someone breaking up their little web of friends—all looking alike, talking alike, dressing alike, thinking alike—can evoke such emotions as anger, sadness and even fear.

In those interview discussions over the past eight years, pastors, deacons and teachers have confidentially told me they want to change their growth model but they are afraid of the backlash they might get from current members. Can you imagine that? Church leaders are moving through their ministries fearful their members will object to people of different races worshipping alongside them. Later, I will share some data indicating how completely out of touch many of these leaders are with their congregations. The sad reality is many such leaders are imposing their own fears upon a congregation which is actually ready for cross-cultural worship. As I said, the matter of cross-cultural worship is first a leadership issue. Later in this book we will discuss some of those key survey and interview findings, but for now let's get back to the fear issue.

Leaders fear losing their familiar model despite its ineffectiveness. They cling to the homogeneous model because they cannot see themselves gaining expertise in a new model. They fear losing what they have—their familiar and ineffective model. However, many leaders also fear gaining what they do not currently have. This may be more tragic a line of thinking than the fear of losing their homogeneous models. To understand this logic, we should look at why leaders do not extend their ministries or encourage their members to extend themselves beyond the self-erected barriers of race and ethnicity.

So what is it that some Christian groups perceive about other Christian groups that would make them avoid cross-cultural interaction and investment? From the scores of pastors, deacons and teachers with whom I have discussed this topic, I draw the conclusion fear has led to prejudice, and this has led to avoidance, and this has led back to fear, and this pattern has repeated itself in a vicious cycle. There is a logic, used by some church leaders, which follows a most peculiar line. I have "heard" so many negative things about "those people." I must avoid too much interaction with them. I must "protect" my family and the flock from them because they are dangerous and so are their ways. I admit, I really don't know much about them. I even admit I could be wrong about them. However, I just cannot take the risk with the spiritual well-being of those whom the Lord has entrusted to me. This line of logic as tragic, but it is also true of far too many in leadership positions within the church.

So what do they fear gaining? Many of our leaders fear gaining what other groups have and their ways of worshipping. If you want to hear a rich discussion among Christians, put a Caucasian and an African American together in conversation over the role of music in a worship service. Many African Americans see predominately white congregations as having the most boring and sterile music imaginable. Though technically and scripturally strong, this music is viewed as lacking emotive strength. It would, no doubt, be mentioned that these songs engage the mind, but they do not engage the spirit. "They do not move me" may be a comment you could expect to hear. When thinking about the typical African American worship music, a Caucasian might view such music as shallow. Perhaps the conversation would reveal a perception the music is only part of the problem. One might point out how the reaction to the music is often more alarming than the music itself. Often, the African American will sing along, clap aloud, raise their hands, or move about in the pews or seats. In doing so, they would "fail" to preserve what some see as the imagery of worship—that is piety and composure.

I have heard this basic conversation many times. So many times, I can almost predict the words and phrases each person will use. Interesting to me, is the fact that often such discord arises in the face of two startling realities: the two groups often sing the same songs, and oftentimes one or both of the people speaking has never been in a church mostly comprised of the demographic group they are criticizing. Actually, the parties engaging in these conversations often have no real insight or experience in what they are talking about. Yet, they defend the rightness of "their way" and the wrongness of "any other way" with fierce determination.

So many leaders fear racial reconciliation among Christians and cross-cultural worship among all believers on the basis of prejudice and hearsay. When leaders exhibit such fear, they no doubt teach it in their formal and informal interactions with other believers. This perpetuates the pattern of segregation we find so prevalent in our churches. In this example, both groups may fear "gaining" the so-called worship style of the other group. In this way, they fear gaining what they do not have.

Some fear gaining what they do not have because they have come to believe that what they have, that is, their way of "doing church" is the best way. In this thinking, all other models for doing church are inferior. Great energy develops to define the way things are done within the group. These become the standards for worshipping and fellowshipping together. To keep their way in tact many congregations have had to build a wall of definition around their way of operating together as a body. Often, over time, all members of a particular group conform to the pattern of "how we do things around here." In other words, members buy into the culture of the congregation with whom they worship. In the context of racial division in the church, it is interesting how one group can literally fear interaction with another because they may "pick up" something undesirable from the other group. This is like avoiding someone who has a contagious virus. But is this any way to treat another believer?

The Fallacy of Affinity

To some of you, the concept of one Christian literally fearing interaction with another Christian is a foreign idea. You may even be appalled to hear such a thing happens among believers. While I appreciate your innocence, I must assure you this happens more often than many in the church would care to admit. Perhaps this next point will help bridge your understanding of the fear of reconciliation and cross-cultural worship. You see, underlying the fear of racial reconciliation is the fallacy of affinity.

Now what is affinity? An affinity is an inherent similarity. Some of the most important and relevant affinities are race, ethnicity, age and gender. Here is how it works: many Christians believe the way to grow the church is through the extension of natural affinity groups. The twentieth-century church growth specialists, such as Donald McGavran, were proponents of this growth strategy. The idea is simple. If people are more comfortable with "their own" people, then why buck against this fact. Instead, we should leverage the natural tendency for birds of a feather to flock together. We should encourage Black Christians to focus their efforts in Black communities. We should enable the efforts of Chinese Christians to witness among other Chinese groups. We should engage White Christians in ministry toward others of European decent. This is logical, right?

After all, aren't people more comfortable with other people who have the same background as they? Freely I admit it is often more comfortable to associate in a group comprised of people with a common affinity. I just wonder if we are somehow missing the point. Jesus never called Christians to faith on a promise of being comfortable. It seems to me Jesus more often warned that Christian faith would create discomfort for the believer. Jesus said, "If any man will follow me, let him take up his cross daily and follow me." He warned that faith in him would challenge pre-existing relationships. When one comes to Christ, he or she may face rejection by their former affinity group, even their familial group.

In fairness, however, we must acknowledge that scholars like McGavran did have a point. It is true churches could grow in America and elsewhere by focusing on affinities. This was also a practical choice. Many of the communities across America were racially segregated, and racial tension was often on the brink of eruption. Fear of racial strife seemed to loom over the society and the church. It was practical, if not merely convenient; to avoid the stresses of working across races when there was ready access to non-Christians of the same race. It was clearly expedient, even safe, to pursue those in the segregated neighborhood with the message of Christ.

In America, affinities were also strengthened by the struggle for individual identity. American society was forged, in some part, by the idea of rugged individualism which gave sway to such philosophies as "pull yourself up by your own bootstraps" and the idea of the "self-made" man. Rugged individualism helped to fuel the women's liberation movement. The quest for individual identity was and is very strong in America and elsewhere. Just notice how people present themselves. We see more behavior designed to attract attention. People dress in extreme garb; pierce, mark and expose their bodies, and do anything they can think of to escape the mainstream of society's expectations for them. This is all about individualism and it is a powerful force in shaping the behavior of people—especially young people.

I have come to appreciate the power of individualism in a different way as I live and work in the Eastern Hemisphere. Eastern cultures are less driven by the forces of individual expression. Although it is slowly changing, eastern cultures like Chinese, Japanese, Korean, and Southeast Asian people groups still emphasize conformity. Unlike American culture, eastern cultures prioritize the needs of the society over the needs of the individual. I do not know if one approach is any better than the other. On the one hand you have individualism where society encourages people to do their own thing or to have it their way. Remember the old Burger King jingle . . . "Hold the pickles, hold the lettuce, special orders don't upset us; all we ask is that you let us have it your way. Have it your way, have it your way, have it your way at Burger King." This jingle tapped into the insight of individual expression as an influencer of behavior.

The peculiar thing about individualism is that individuals still seek out for affinities. Yes people want to be viewed as "different" but they simultaneously seem to look for others who are being different in the exact same way. Even the person who is avoiding conformity is seeking an affinity with others. You see, people are social creatures. We have a need to belong. So whilst our desire is often to express our individual needs or preferences, the power of affinities can be a stronger factor in our behavior than we know or are willing to admit. So why do I say there is a fallacy in affinity?

Here is the challenge with all this focus on affinities. The face of our communities is changing, and the face of Christianity must also change. Communities are far less segregated in America and in every large city around the world. Within the church, Christianity is developing from a mostly white and mostly western religious affinity to an increasingly multi-cultural, multi-lingual and global body of believers. So the communities we serve look very different today from what was typical even a few decades ago. In the 1970's segregation was still the order of the day. In the twenty-first century, it is difficult to find strictly segregated communities, especially in the largest urban centers where most people will live. It is, therefore, difficult to maintain a segregated approach to church growth. To maintain segregation, churches must consciously avoid segments of their neighboring communities. Like the priest and the Levite in the parable of the Good Samaritan, they must consciously pass by "the lost" and dying neighbor in their own neighborhood in search of someone in their affinity group. This is where affinity begins to break down as a strategy for church growth. Where is the fallacy in affinity? The fallacy is that the pursuit of affinity groups will lead to continual growth of the church of Jesus Christ. Instead of growing, the church will become less and less effective as we pass by our neighbors looking for people just like ourselves. The church will lose its relevance as current congregants reject the duplicity implied in working and associating across cultures outside the church but worshipping within a cultural jail cell that seems to keep squeezing them into a small box of racial segregation they no longer want or understand.

Indeed there is a clear pattern toward further diversity in the world-wide body of believers. Not only are Christians more diverse demographically, but these believers, with different racial backgrounds are living in ever-closer proximity. It is incumbent upon the church, if we are to continue growing, to unlearn the separatist philosophies and traditions that have led us to pursue racial homogeneity as a primary strategy for church growth in the twenty-first century.[28] Not only that, but it is essential for churches to invest in cross-cultural worship if we are to grow spiritually healthy churches. Maintaining racial segregation will mean the church must perpetuate the very barriers we are commanded by Christ to break through. We have already proven that Jesus Christ broke down the walls of separation between races. To preserve segregation we will have to reconstruct those walls. I don't know about you, but I do not see the value of working to redo that which Christ has so sacrificially undone. I do not choose to work against Christ and his purpose for the church. The fallacy of affinity is that it causes us to be at odds with Christ whom we are committed to follow, obey and serve.

I know some of you are thinking I may be too extreme in my effort to reject the strategy of affinity. You may argue many churches do not set out to maintain segregation. It just somehow naturally happens. Your church may indeed be completely segregated. You may argue this is not because of some great intentionality. You may take offense to the implication of this discussion. As you think about it, perhaps you recognize segregation in the church, like in the larger society is driven by intentional effort. I hate to be in your face about this, but maybe this is what is needed to break you and me out of the pattern. You may be discovering how this whole discussion could imply your church is segregated because of racial or ethnic bias. Perhaps your mind is working along this line of thinking: Hold on Witherspoon! Are you implying I am biased toward people of other races?

I will have you know I am not prejudiced toward anyone inside or outside the church. Some of my best friends are from other races.

I have heard this line of reasoning so many times over the years. People often present their cross-cultural friendships as evidence they are not biased in their attitudes toward other races. This is de facto used as justification for segregated worship. Upon further examination, many who offer this explanation about their personal attitude toward other races have few to no active cross-cultural relationships. In such a conversation, they discover how wedded they really are to the affinity strategy. I used to think it was important to help expose this inconsistency in others so they could address their tendency and expand their circle of friends to include people from other races. I thought this would be the key factor leading to cross-cultural worship and racial reconciliation in the church. The problem, however, is not whether they have cross-cultural relationships or friendships. The problem is cross-cultural friendship can have little or no impact upon the propagation of cross-cultural worship. Remember, we have seen how the New Testament clearly directs us toward cross-cultural worship, but many are making excuses for why this cannot happen. Some are arguing for why this should not happen. We have seen how segregation in the church is often driven by a fear of racial reconciliation. We have noted how segregated churches stand on a foundation of the fallacious strategy of affinity-based growth. Again, proponents of this strategy sometimes argue they are neither against cross-cultural worship, nor do they get in the way of cross-cultural worship. They take the attitude if it will happen, then let it happen. They do not invest in cross-cultural worship, but they do not discourage it either. They sometimes even present their cross-cultural friendships as evidence of their openness to cross-cultural relationships. These friendships may or may not exist, but regardless of their existence, friendship is not enough to drive cross-cultural worship.

Cross-cultural Friendship is Insufficient

To illustrate the limitation of cross-cultural friendship as a catalyst to cross-cultural worship, let us look at a few examples. The story is told of Dr. Martin Luther King's childhood experience in cross-cultural friendship. When Dr. King was a youngster his family moved to a new community. Over the summer, while on break from school, he met another young boy and they became fast friends. Like typical children with newfound friends, the boys played together every day. They would go over to each other's homes and they would roam about the neighborhood playing games and enjoying one another's company. This went on for weeks.

One day, near the end of the summer break, young Martin went over to see and play with his friend. When he arrived and knocked at the door of his friend's home, the boy's mother answered the door. She told young Martin that her son would not be coming out to play with him today. She went on to tell Martin how they should stop playing together. It was okay, she said, when it was summer time. Now they were about to start school, and it was best they simply break off their friendship and go their separate ways.

Martin went on to other things that day, and the boys did not play together anymore. I often think about this little story and I find it instructive in so many ways. You see, the boys met and established a friendship on the basis of common interests. They cultivated that friendship into a deeper friendship, and were content to carry on as friends indefinitely. After all, this is what little boys (and little girls) tend to do when they meet new boys and girls. It did not matter much to these two boys one was Black and the other was White. They were more interested in being friends than in national politics and race relations. They were not trying to make any kind of statement by playing together, they were just being friends.

However, when adversity came into their friendship, it could not withstand the forces which sought to sever ties and break bonds. In a moment, their innocent little friendship was nullified by a mother who decided her son and young Martin would be better off if they just stayed and played among their own racial affinity group. I find this story, and so many like it, tragic. It is tragic on many fronts. First, it is tragic to realize the sincerity of the young White boy's mother who probably was just being honest about the cold realities of a harsh, segregated society who would cast a collective frown upon this cross-cultural relationship. That mother knew in her heart the boys would be ridiculed and their friendship would likely meet with disdain from both Blacks and Whites alike. Second, it is a great tragedy that both sets of parents and both these boys were not ready or willing to defy this social challenge. I don't know if I would have, or if you would have, challenged the situation. I just know it is tragic to see the separatist philosophy of affinity-based segregation claimed a victory that day. In America's Deep South and in the 1940's no less, it could have been fatal to stand against this challenge. Third, and perhaps most important, it is tragic to see the frailty of friendship. These two boys probably had a genuine friendship built upon mutual interest, trust and respect. They probably shared secrets, shared meals, and maybe even shared their dreams. However, the truth is their friendship was insufficient to carry them through the challenge of racial affinity. They were defined by their race and it was their race which precluded them from pursuing a genuine friendship beyond that eventful summer.

My observation is that even the innocence of childhood friendships is insufficient to overcome the force of affinity-based segregation. Let me share how this point has also been highlighted in my own life. When I was growing up, I was a pretty good kid, that is, I usually stayed out of trouble and avoided the kinds of activities which would bring embarrassment to my family. I grew up in poor and middle-class neighborhoods so I saw poverty and all the trappings of typical impoverished communities. I was always very opinionated and I never walked away from a good debate or argument. At times I would get into little arguments with other kids, and sometimes these little squabbles would escalate into fist fights. In my neighborhood, this was not unusual. It seemed fights were a way for young boys to blow off steam and to establish their place in the neighborhood hierarchy: you know, tough kids at the top and weak kids at the bottom.

In our neighborhood system, you could never allow another boy to take advantage of you or embarrass you without getting even with the offender. When conflict arose, there would be an imbalance or an uncertainty in our system until the matter was somehow resolved. For example, a tougher kid may be challenged for his position of authority by a smaller or weaker kid. This type of challenge would need to be sorted so we all knew who our leaders would be. A good fist fight usually settled these types of disputes and brought equilibrium back to the neighborhood. Growing up, I was always average in size or smaller than my peer group. So I needed compensating factors, of which I had several. One of the ways I compensated was by working harder academically and getting extremely good grades in school. When I would be challenged to fights, I could talk my way out of it, reframe the challenge into an intellectual one versus a physical one, or apply one of my other compensating factors. Despite this tool kit for avoiding fights, I would sometimes have to settle matters with an old fashioned fist fight.

When I reflect on all the fist fights I had growing up, it strikes me that the most important ones, the fights which had a profound impact upon my life, were rooted in racial prejudice. These fights were part of a bigger plot in which I, and those little boys whom I fought, were defending with violent zeal the race-based fallacy of affinity. Let me explain using three fights I had with White kids in school.

The first such cross-cultural fight I remember was in fifth grade. This was during the time when communities were still figuring out how to deal with "busing" in the southern state of Florida where I grew up. Each day, I traveled by bus to an elementary school across town in a predominately white neighborhood. This was part of a national effort to break down racial segregation in public schools.

As mentioned earlier, I was a bit smaller than most of my classmates during this time. In the late morning, the bell would ring signaling it was time for my class to go outside for physical education or "PE." Each day the bell would ring and there would be a huge crowd of fifth-graders rushing out to the PE field to find out what athletic challenge we would face and enjoy today. At age ten or eleven we always seemed to have plenty of energy and enthusiasm. We also seemed to see the PE period as a natural time to let off steam in the spirit of competition. Looking back, I now realize it was also a time when boys could show off their strength and endurance in front of the girls. So everything became a competition among the boys.

One of the most interesting competitions was to see who would win the race to be first in line as we assembled for PE class. Now here is how it worked. There were eight car tires buried halfway in the ground; they were numbered one through eight and lined up in succession about three feet apart. At the beginning of the year, we were advised that the first person in each line would be "leader" for the day. I was smaller than most of the other boys, but I was also a faster runner. Over time, I and my other Black classmates from the neighborhood would outrun all the other kids and take the first position in front of four of the numbered tires, leaving four spaces for others to take the lead position. Over time, a clear pattern formed, and everyone seemed to settle into an unspoken understanding this was the way it was supposed to be. So for weeks Tommy Terry, Michael Terry, Yancey Cooper and I would get to the lead position at "our" tires and assume our position as leaders. The role allowed us to direct the activity of all the other students in our line. Usually, we would lead in exercises and in whatever drills or sporting activities the PE teacher had for us to do. Of course, in the process of leading, we had the opportunity to show off our skills for the girls in the class. Though the four of us were Black, we were keen to earn the attention of any girl—Black or White.

One day, the bell rang and I was challenged for the lead position at my tire by a new kid who had been in our class for only a couple weeks. His name was Billy and he was considerably taller than I. I did not realize he was vying for my spot until we had nearly reached the tire, so we arrived in a virtual tie for the first position. Immediately, there was tension in the air. The tension was driven, in part, by the fact everyone knew this was "my tire" and this was exacerbated by the fact Billy was a White kid. So here we were pushing and shoving for the first position and both claiming to have arrived first. It was a real moment of truth! With hardly a direct word being spoken we squared off for a head to head confrontation. Suddenly, Billy charged at me and I ducked onto one knee. Billy's forward momentum propelled him over my shoulder just as I was standing up so he took a hard tumble to the ground. It looked like a brilliant judo or wrestling move on my part, and while Billy lay startled on the ground all the kids erupted into laughter.

Just then the PE teacher arrived and we all straightened up as though nothing had happened. Afterward, Billy was embarrassed to have been thrust to the ground by this smaller kid, and I was seen as a "hero" among my crew of friends from the neighborhood. Billy, it turns out, had always used his size as an advantage and he had in a short time at our school, established himself as a bit of a bully. Billy never knew it, but I ducked that day out of fearful and instinctive reaction. I never let on to him or anyone else I was afraid of getting hurt in that brief exchange. Thankfully, Billy never sought to get even with me through violence, but our relationship was always strained from that point forward. We sort of avoided each other and figured out how to co-exist without provoking one another. After the fifth grade, Billy and I went to different Middle Schools, so we never saw each other again.

My second important cross-cultural fight was in the seventh grade. Our family had moved to the North side of town and I went to a new Junior High School. Again, this school was integrated due to a program of busing kids from varying neighborhoods. My best friend in school was a White kid named Alexander Laufenberg who was in several classes with me. We hung out together at school and sometimes got together after school. When I wasn't hanging out with Alex I was probably with my football or basketball teammates. I loved sports when I was young.

Now my favorite sport was basketball, and I made the school basketball team as a starting forward. Our practices were exhausting as we rehearsed our offensive and defensive plays hundreds of times, executed countless skill drills, and ran sprints and "suicides" for hours each day after school. A suicide is a type of conditioning exercise where players line up on the baseline at one end of the basketball court. At the sound of the coach's whistle, the players run and touch the free throw line then sprint back to the baseline; they run to the half court line and back to the base line; they run to the far free throw line and back to the baseline; then run all the way to the opposite baseline and back. Each complete run of this drill is about 500 feet, and after about ten of these you feel like you are dying. This is why they are called suicides.

One day we had another of those exhaustive practices and we were all so tired we could hardly think straight. Our drill and play execution began to get sloppy and before long we were making mistakes at every turn. The coach got so frustrated he walked out of the gymnasium, drove off and left the team captains in charge of straightening us out. Well, we kept on running the plays poorly and it was one of the worst practice sessions any of us had ever seen. On one play I was facing and defending another player and trying to keep him from catching a pass. When I turned to look at the other kid who was trying to pass the ball to the guy I was defending, all I could see was the ball getting larger and larger in front of my face. All at once, the ball smacked me right in the kisser. My whole head rang like a bell! Stunned, I fell to one knee and tears welled up in the corners of my eyes as surprise gave way to pain—excruciating pain. When I rubbed my hand across my face, it seemed I could still feel the impression of the grooves in the basketball imprinted on my head.

It seemed clear to me that my team mate, who happened to be white, threw the ball and hit me in the face on purpose. I was furious! I directed the most piercing scowl imaginable toward him, and told him we would settle this after practice. I stormed into the locker room, though practice was not yet over, and I showered and waited for the rest of the team to be dismissed. When they arrived in the locker room, I was still upset and the atmosphere was tense. The other kid and I exchanged no words, but everyone knew we would have to settle this according to the time-honored tradition—a fist fight. Of course, as an adult, I find this a barbaric way to resolve issues. However, when I was growing up this is the way it was done. Part of me says, "Thank God" we only used fist fights to settle disputes. Today, kids no longer fight with fists, they bring weapons to school and shoot and stab their classmates to death. Both approaches are wrong, but one gives both parties a chance to do the right thing next time. The other always ends with tragic consequence.

When everyone had showered, following our disastrous practice session, we all stepped outside into the warm Florida afternoon sun. Just outside the locker room, there was a long strip of grass between the outer wall of the gymnasium building and a chain link fence bordering the school property. Almost ceremoniously we all stepped onto the grassy area and dropped our gym bags to the ground. The two of us squared off, and the crowd encircled us almost completely divided along racial lines. The White kids were on one side and everyone else was on the other side. With tensions high and the crowd egging us on, we began to rumble.

Soon I took advantage of the other kid by taking him to the ground and pinning his arms beneath my knees. I am not proud of it, but I managed a decisive victory over the other young man. My teammate had braces so his face was soon bloodied by shots to the mouth. He fought back initially, but eventually surrendered. We stood up and I insisted he apologize in front of everyone present. I hardly remember the moments of the actual brawl, but I clearly recall the chanting and encouragement of the Black kids who saw this as a victory of our side over "the Whites." After the fight, things returned to normal and we played the rest of the basketball season without further incident. Somehow our fight had released us all from the tension and the need to fight anymore among ourselves.

The third and final cross-cultural fight happened when I was in the tenth grade. After completing my high school freshman year in New York, I returned to Florida and the community in which I had grown up. Over the summer before the school year started, I rekindled old relationships with many of my old classmates and we had a great time hanging out and dreaming together about what we would do as upper-classmen once the school year started.

Once school started, I was so motivated to be back among my friends and in very familiar surroundings. The tenth grade was an outstanding year for me academically and socially. I had a great group of friends who all had bright future potential as athletes, entertainers or college students. I had a nice girlfriend and a great social life. You could say I had it all. I was so into my friends and our little social circles that I rarely got into any situations where there were arguments or fights. I had moved away from settling disputes by fist fight and opted for diplomacy instead. Any time there was animosity or jealousy between me and another kid, I would resort to verbal sparring and I would ridicule physical altercations as a base form of animalistic territorialism. Even if someone would challenge me to a physical contest, I would challenge them to a public display of our report cards and progress reports. This would diffuse matters and avoid any intended aggression. I had mastered the art of staying out of fights.

It was near the end of the school year, and I was on top of the world. My grades were stellar, my life was in control, and I was extremely active in church and civic programs. With about ten days left in school, I was in PE class near the end of the school day. We had been divided into teams for competitive basketball on the school's outdoor basketball courts. There were eight goals so we could play four full-court games simultaneously. I was on a team playing with boys I knew and with whom I had grown up. We were winning the game and having a wonderful time of it. Our opponents were kids we knew but they were not part of our little clique of regular friends and associates.

As the game progressed, the scores got closer and the competition really intensified. I don't know if you have ever played basketball, but it is very common to experience a little "trash talking" during a competitive game of hoops. This game was no exception. At one point, I and the guy I was guarding began trading baskets. He would get the ball and make a shot, and then I would get the ball and return the favor. All the while we were talking trash. He would make a shot and exclaim, "I'm unstoppable." I would make a shot and retort, "You can't guard me." This went back and forth for a while. Then I took a shot and made it. I looked at him and said, "In your face" and turned to run up court. While I was running toward the other goal, I could feel someone approaching rapidly behind me.

Before I could turn around, the kid who I was guarding came up behind me and punched me right in the nose. I had never been hit so hard. It was worse than the feeling I experienced when hit by the basketball in the seventh grade. Again I was stunned! My nose was bleeding profusely. When I saw the blood, I went after the other kid with a fury. We made a genuine mess of each other. He ended up with a broken jaw and I suffered a broken nose. It was terrible. Finally, the PE instructors and the other kids separated us and we were taken to the principal's office.

So there you have it. I have shared the stories of three fights I had as a youth. Why would I share these stories? After all, I'm a preacher of the gospel. You are probably thinking I don't want to go to church with this guy or hear him preach. If I criticized one of his sermons would he get upset and challenge me to a fist fight? I assure you, I will do no such thing. I am not proud of these fights, but I share them because they have been a source of great learning for me. I share them because the lessons I have learned from these incidents help to illustrate why friendship is not enough to bring about racial reconciliation and why friendship will not necessarily drive cross-cultural worship.

I have learned two key lessons from these childhood altercations. First, I have learned to acknowledge my own prejudices and unhealthy biases toward others. Second, I found out I was sometimes more committed to preserving affinity-based relationships than to doing the right thing. These two personal insights come in light of a very important contextual point—I became a Christian in the fifth grade. As a Christian, I should never have been in any of these altercations. Thankfully, that tenth-grade fight was my last. Let me now share the three insights with a focus on what I have learned about myself.

I have learned to acknowledge my own prejudice and bias toward others. Like many who grew up in the United States, I saw the world through a racial lens. Of course, my world was not very big. For the most part, my world was really a US-centric construct comprised of Blacks and Whites and the occasional other person from a Hispanic or Asian background. Often, my cross-cultural perspective was just a reflection of what was evident in my neighborhood. It was admittedly a narrow view of the world, but it was not an uncommon view. Too many Americans, in my day, had this narrow view of what it meant to operate across cultures. Shaped by the lingering impact of slavery, it seemed the whole of American society viewed race relations and cross-cultural exchange as a simple matter of Black and White. This is not dissimilar from the Old Testament saints who saw the whole world as a simple matter of Jew and Gentile.

When I examine those three childhood fist fights, I now realize they had a common thread. Each of those fights was, in some way, enabled by my own personal prejudice toward White people. Let me explain.

In that fifth grade fight, I would easily have relinquished the leadership position had Billy been a Black kid. I would probably have given the other kid a high-five handshake and congratulated him. I may even have seen the whole event as a smart, heads-up move by the other Black kid to arrive first at the tire. My learning would probably have been about staying focused on reaching the goal and being more aware of what was happening around me.

Instead, when I saw Billy was White, I knew immediately I could never stand for him to displace me from such a leadership position. What drove such a distinction in my reaction? It was my own twisted perspective which sought to divide the world into Black and White. It was my own failure to get beyond the apparent limitations and to create possibilities from the situation. In short, it was my prejudice. Prejudice is an interesting word. It essentially means to pre-judge or to judge someone before getting the relevant facts. This is exactly what I was doing to Billy. I assumed he also saw our little situation as a racial challenge. I never asked him what he thought or how he felt. I simply assumed it was a power struggle with the outcome defining a winner and a loser, or more specifically, a winning and a losing race of people.

Of course, it could be true that Billy also saw it as a racial standoff. The fact is, however, his viewpoint could not absolve me from somehow figuring out how to do the right thing. Perhaps it is good I do not know what Billy was thinking at the time because in a way it doesn't matter what he was thinking. You see, my doing the right thing can never be contingent upon whether the other fellow does the right thing or not.

I was prejudiced against my teammate in the seventh grade basketball practice. I never stopped to verify his intentions when I was hit with that ball. I assumed he did it on purpose, partly because he did not immediately apologize, and partly because my mind was conditioned to be suspicious of White folks. I now find it ironic to have carried such racial suspicion, even when my best friend was Alexander Laufenberg. By leaving the basketball court without getting clear on the facts, I set up the conditions which led to the fight. I declared we would settle it after practice. I allowed myself to be alone in the locker room, without truly knowing whether he was sorry, and getting angrier by the moment. I was allowing my prejudice to define the set of possible remedies to our little problem. Whether or not he slapped my face with that ball on purpose, I failed to turn the other cheek.

Again, in the tenth grade brawl, my prejudice appeared. Sadly, I felt justified in this situation. After all, the kid hit me first. He made it physical when he hit me first. I was simply defending myself and defending my manhood. In my neighborhood economy, no one was expected to take such a blow without retaliation. I acted in self defense, right? I wish it were that simple. Clearly, I did not have to fight him back. However, even after all these years of reflection, I still feel the tug of prejudice, racial affinity and teenage machismo which drove me into an all out brawl. I did not see a class mate who got upset with me, I saw a White kid who tried to make me feel less of a man. I saw all that with no discussion and no interest in the other fellow.

In all three instances I was acting upon a personal bias—a prejudice—which I felt was fully justified. I thought I had a right to be prejudiced because of all that had happened to me and every other African American down through the years. I had a chip the size of a railroad tie on my shoulder and it interfered with my ability to embrace others across racial barriers. I have now learned to acknowledge this bias. By doing so, I can establish a cross-cultural relationship based upon true feelings. I can also work to build trust and transparency with others. This has been liberating for me. I have, over the years, been slowly whittling away at the chip on my shoulder.

The second thing I learned from these fights was the enormous weight I had put on affinity-based relationships as a determinant for how I engaged others. I tended to view all relationships through a racial lens. Prospective relationships were filtered through this lens. With other African Americans the filtering was instantaneous and required no real thought on my part. When I encountered other races, especially White people, the process took considerably more effort. With Blacks I began with an implied trust. They were cool with me until they proved otherwise. With Whites it was a different story. I started these relationships with skepticism. They had to prove themselves trustworthy.

Naturally, when I encountered White people in situations where time seemed to deny us the chance to know each other, I defaulted to skepticism. This happened in each of these three fights. Strangely, in each fight there was an unspoken social norm at play: loyalty to your race must always be evident. I had bought into this framework. Early on, I came to believe it was important. Eventually, I believed it was right.

Somehow the pressure and responsibility of representing my race was always upon me. I was always sensitive to how my action would be received and perceived by those in my racial affinity group. I was not unique in this feeling of responsibility. I think many of the kids from my neighborhood would have felt the same way. I suspect the kids from other affinity groups often felt this pressure too.

In the fifth grade situation, I quickly came to the conclusion the Black kids were counting on me to stand against Billy. I had it in my mind the group wanted me to fight for my lead spot. In seconds I was into this competition with Billy. But it was about much more than Billy or me. This battle was about Black folks' right to lead. I had heaped a lot of pressure upon myself. I cared about what my affinity group would think of me. If I had failed to stand up I would be rejected and ridiculed. If I fought Billy head to head and won, then I would have done what was expected of me.

In the seventh grade altercation I could not believe this guy had the audacity to hit me with that ball. I was instantly thinking about the implications of it. I knew, for example, if I let it go, my Black teammates would have considered me a wimp who failed to stand up and fight. In the economy of my neighborhood the fight was a clear next step. There was no way I was going to let the other Black kids down. They needed to know I cared as much for "my people" as I cared for myself. If I fought and beat the kid, it would send a strong signal to the White kids, and it would strengthen solidarity among the Black kids. Again, I was completely committed to delivering against the expectations of my affinity group. Almost nothing else mattered in the situation. I never considered getting kicked off the team. I never thought about the cost to his parents of my ruining the guy's braces. All other considerations and potential consequences paled in comparison to my focus on winning favor among the Black kids.

In the tenth grade fight I immediately felt the pressure to defeat this White kid who was so bold as to strike me in front of my boys. Though he had "sucker-punched" me I was determined not to allow him to make a sucker of me. He brought the fight to me, and I was not going to back down. I felt it would be a slap in the face to all the African American kids who were present. I was bleeding profusely, but that did not deter me from defending my personal honor and the standing of my affinity group.

Some might say I am being pretty tough on myself in this book. In some respects I was operating according to the unspoken rules of cross-cultural engagement. I was operating within the expectations of the larger society. I could probably lay legitimate claim to that excuse. The problem is I had become, like many of my contemporaries, more attune to how other Blacks would interpret my action, than to how the Lord would see me. My choices, when under fire, would be designed to gain the favor of my affinity group. I pursued this acceptance to the exclusion of any consideration of how the Lord would receive my chosen actions. To some degree it is unrealistic to expect children to navigate the challenges of social segregation and racial prejudice. However, it is appropriate to expect Christians, even young ones, to be guided more by what is right than by who is watching.

Again, I am not proud of these childhood fights, but the learning has been rich. I have learned to acknowledge my personal bias toward Caucasians. This has helped me to develop honest and lasting relationships across this racial barrier. I hope you are able to be honest with yourself and others respecting any prejudices you may have. Looking back upon these childhood days, I can also see the power of racial affinity groups. I see many people driven by the desire to demonstrate loyalty to their particular affinity group.

The biggest insight for me has been realizing that friendship is insufficient to drive cross-cultural worship. My personal experience illustrates the power of the affinity group loyalty. I had White friends throughout my youth. In some cases, I had strong and long-standing friendships with White kids. However, these friendships did not keep me from getting into these fights. When it came time to act under pressure, I acted to preserve my standing within my affinity group. I did not think about my White friends and apply the benefits of these friendships to the three boys with whom I fought. When the going got tough I defaulted to my affinity.

LET US END SPIRITUAL SEGREGATION

To this point, we have discussed the conditions of segregated worship. However, the purpose of this book is not simply to cite the condition, but to provide a Biblical approach to remedy the issue of segregated worship within the Church. I think a case has been made for cross-cultural worship. We have seen the clear Biblical mandate which should give us the internal motivation to change. We have also seen how shifting demographics will put external pressure on segregated worship. When I discuss cross-cultural worship with church leaders, they eventually tend to agree with the basis for change. However, they also tend to stop short of implementing changes because they do not know where to begin. They have been conditioned socially and trained academically to drive worship in a homogeneous racial and cultural context. This next section is meant to provide some of the "how to" behind cross-cultural worship. Here I will explain two tools I have developed to help churches move forward in cross-cultural worship: the Cross-Cultural Worship Model and the Readiness Assessment Survey.

Introducing the Cross-Cultural Worship Model

The Cross-Cultural Worship Model (CCW) is the crystallization of what I have learned about the way to develop and sustain cross-cultural worship. The model is straightforward and has three key strategic components: integration, penetration and reconciliation. These three elements combine to form the stages of cross-cultural relationship development required to bring racial diversity to life in the church. The principles also hold true in bridging other divisions such as age, gender, ethnicity, etc.

It is important to remind you I am writing to Christians and the model is about cross-cultural worship within the Christian Church. Though some of the findings and the methodology may be effective in a secular context, I am not putting forward an answer to the broader social issues surrounding diversity and race relations.

In this section, I will explain each of the three strategic components of the model. Central to cross-cultural worship is the cross. Hence the entire model revolves around and is entirely enabled by the cross. I have found the model to hold true in many settings involving different church sizes, varying combinations of affinity groups, and multiple locations. The model is simple, but it is powerfully effective. Later, I will share several examples where I have seen the model applied in real life situations. Learning from these experiences has reinforced the model's validity and value.

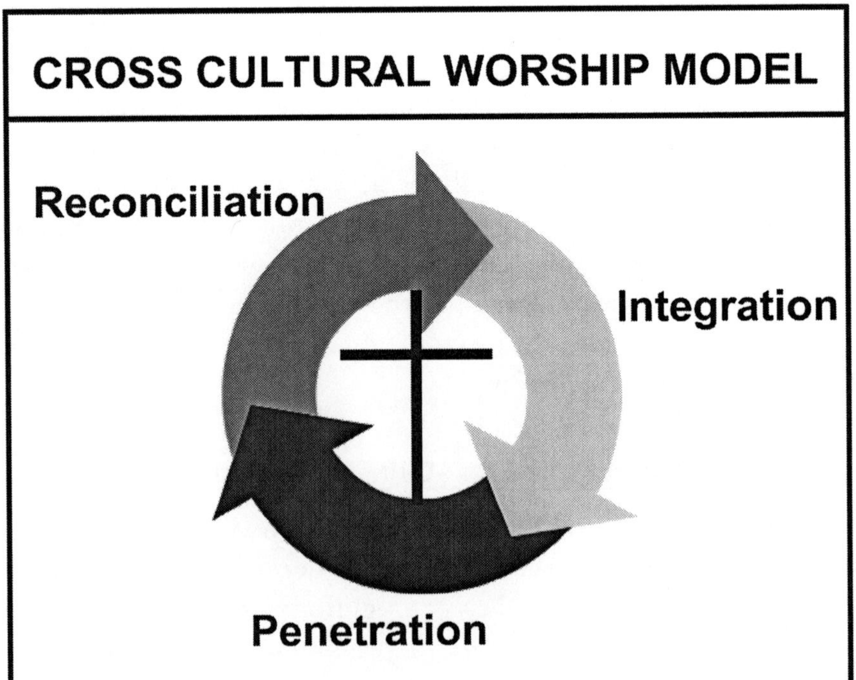

The first stage of the CCW Model is called "integration." Integration, for the purpose of this discussion, is the conscious effort to bring different races into physical proximity for corporate worship and fellowship. It may sound simple or even obvious, but there will be no "cross-cultural" worship if the different racial groups within the Christian community of faith do not come together. So our first strategic choice must be to bring Christians together across racial and other barriers to worship and praise our Lord. No doubt, integration was the intent of the early church. There is no teaching in the New Testament which supports segregated churches.

Consider the Apostle Paul's statement to the church at Rome. He said, "Accept one another, then, just as Christ accepted you, in order to bring praise to God. For I tell you that Christ has become a servant of the Jews on behalf of God's truth, to confirm the promises made to the patriarchs so that the Gentiles may glorify God." Notice the picture of unity Paul establishes in this statement. He says, "Accept one another" or in the King James translation, "receive" one another. We should note two things about this statement. Firstly, Paul writes this in the present imperative tense which means it is a command to be carried out immediately upon reading. It is not given as a suggestion or an option to be considered. Paul's intent was for the church to receive or accept all people no matter how different their background or heritage may be. It can clearly be inferred the Roman church was struggling with acceptance of certain believers. Paul speaks directly to the issue and insists the church change this behavior right away.

Secondly, this statement reflects the image of one person welcoming another into his presence or into his home. The words used here, and translated receive or accept means to take to oneself. I see this idea as a powerful expression of Paul's command to the Church that we welcome all Christians to the faithful worship of Jesus Christ. Don't miss this—Paul is speaking to the Church about relationships within the Church. The broader context is about strong and weak brethren. Strength or weakness, in this context, is about the variation in what Christians believe. In chapter 14, Paul gives examples such as individual attitudes toward holy days and dietary habits. At the beginning of Romans chapter 15 he says, "The strong ought to bear with the failings of the weak." It is in this context Paul commands the Church, in verse 7, to "receive" one another.

You may not see the connection of this to the challenge of cross-cultural integration. I submit to you, though, that individual attitudes, styles and preferences are exactly the sort of thing which precludes cross-cultural worship. As Christians we become wedded to the prevalent attitudes, styles and preferences of our affinity groups. Black folks "prefer" to do church one way and White folks prefer another. Even within the universe of Black Christians, individual preferences and worship styles divide us. Whole churches spring up over the use or non-use of particular instruments in the worship service. So when Paul says in Romans chapter 15, verse 7, that we must receive one another he is speaking to the exact condition we face in the modern church.

Let's look again at this passage. After saying, receive one another, Paul proceeds to quote two Old Testament passages. He quotes King David who said, "I will praise you among the nations" (or among the Gentiles).[29] Then he quotes Moses who said, "Rejoice O nations with his people."[30] Could the Apostle Paul, by quoting these two Old Testament passages, be implying the church at Rome should reflect the unity of praise called for by these two stalwarts of the Jewish faith? I think this is exactly what he is implying. The challenge for us, in the modern Church, is to bring this unity of praise to life. We must offer our praise "among" the nations and "with" his people. This is the picture of cross-cultural integration.

Recall our definition of integration—it is a conscious effort to bring different people into physical proximity for corporate worship and fellowship. Apart from a conscious effort, the power of affinity-based segregation will hold sway over our churches. Ministries which have endeavored to appeal to more of their communities have learned they must do more than simply desire integration. The inertia of current reality can tend to work against new thinking. People often become comfortable with their current reality and fearful of any change. This is the recipe for extinction.

In nature, certain animals are accustomed to certain specific foods. Their comfort with these foods is built up over generations of repeated behavior. The repetition drives increasing competence, even expertise. Over time, when it comes to finding and eating that particular food, these animals will have a high degree of mastery. In time, their taste is so attuned to this particular food, anything other than this specific food is not fit for consumption. They can eat nothing else. What happens, though, when this food source runs out or the animal is introduced to a new environment? Sadly, some animals faced extinction because they simply would not change.

Man, however, is the most adaptive of all creatures. God has given us the ability to reason at a higher order than other species. With this capacity to reason and subsequent adaptability, we can change our habits and practices to adapt to changes in the environmental conditions. Not only that, but mankind can also alter the environment. We can effect changes in our surroundings to facilitate our continued existence. I am fascinated by the creativity of some cultures and groups in adapting to the environment. In Asia, some wear cone-shaped hats designed to shade their heads and to move large amounts of rain away from their bodies. All this so they can continue to work and live. In the extreme Alaskan winters, Eskimos have learned to fish in frozen-over waterways and to make homes from snow and ice. Again, these creative adaptations enable them to live and work. It seems people are enormously creative when it comes to survival.

I wonder why we lay aside our ability to adapt when we enter the church. We somehow forget how to change ourselves and we lose interest in anything which requires us to adapt a new practice. If you want to see inflexibility and a lack of adaptability suggest something be changed in your church. People want to enjoy routine in church. We want to sit in the same place, sing the same songs, listen to the same messages, fellowship with the same people, and enter and leave the worship service at precisely the same time each week. Change any of these particulars and you will witness the most vigorous objection.

To what are we objecting? We are objecting to change; and in doing so, we invite extinction upon ourselves. We are setting aside all our God-given adaptability in favor of extra-biblical preferences. You see, we often do not get our preferences for where to sit, what to sing, and what instruments to play from the Bible. We get these preferences from generations of repetition. Like the animal whose current food source has become his only food, our current worship styles have become our only way to worship. Any other food is not really food, and any other worship style is not really worship. I don't know about you, but I would rather be part of building up the church than facilitating its demise. Thank God some Christian congregations are seeing the error of getting locked into only one form or style of worship. A great new music is emerging which mingles the more technical western sounds with the harmonious call and response rhythms of the east. Technology is enhancing individual engagement and comprehension of the message. People who at one time were separated in worship are slowly coming together in many of the churches. The change is simply too little and too slow. We must accelerate such changes because they facilitate cross-cultural worship. We must facilitate cross-cultural worship because its alternative is so often driven by artificial means and is inconsistent with the Lord's plan for his church. So a conscious effort is required to bring about a significant change in our condition. We must consciously apply our God-given ability to adapt and to change in order to usher in the era of widespread cross-cultural integration.

To their credit, I already see many church leaders opening their minds to the possibility of a cross-cultural congregation. Indeed, some churches already enjoy a noticeable level of cross-cultural integration. To advance this strategic challenge, I usually advise pastoral teams to get in touch with the current attitudes of their members toward cross-cultural worship. I encourage them to understand how their congregants think about the need to work across cultural barriers. Sadly, I have found some pastors are completely out of touch with where their members are with respect to integrated worship. I have developed a specific tool designed to assess and highlight how in touch church leaders are with their members. I will discuss this tool a bit later.

As part of this strategy, churches should examine the barriers, intended and unintended, which keep people of different racial backgrounds from joining their congregation. It is amazing to see how many walls church folk can erect to overtly or subtly say to whole groups of people "we don't really want you here." For example, some churches position their leaders in front of the church during worship services or in printed material or on the church website. When all these leaders are from only one affinity group, it sends a strong signal to prospective members from other backgrounds they could never lead here. Such a church does not apply the principle of shared leadership modeled by the New Testament church at Antioch. As a result, they unwittingly offend and negatively impact the chances of integrating the congregation of God's people in their place of worship.

There are many, many more examples of simple and complex barriers to entry Christians encounter when they go to a new church. I wonder what kinds of barriers you would find in your church. Here is a little practical exercise for you. Next Sunday when you go to church, imagine you are from another race. Observe how your church "receives" you on Sunday morning. Ask yourself what your church is doing to make other believers from different races a part of the fabric of the ministry. Make a list of all the barriers you can identify then ask why these barriers exist and what it would take to remove them? Looking at your list, ask yourself how seeing these barriers have made you feel? Share your observations with someone in leadership at your church.

Knowing what we have discussed already, I hope you would have a healthy dissatisfaction with the existence of any barrier to cross-cultural worship. Of course, if there are barriers to integration of believers, this must be corrected before we can have any hope of moving to true cross-cultural worship. Indeed, integration is the first step. It is fair to say cross-cultural integration among believers is not easy. If it were, perhaps segregated congregations would be far less prevalent. It is also certain the challenge of such integration is less difficult when the intent to integrate exists in a church's leaders and members. Has your desire for cross-cultural worship been enhanced by our discussion? If so, determine personally to do something about it. Start with your current church body. Find out if your church; at least, mirrors the community it serves in terms of racial composition. This is a reasonable benchmark to set as your minimum expectation. If your church were to truly embrace cross-cultural worship, you may be able to exceed the level of diversity in the immediate community surrounding the church. The fact is many Christians are looking for churches that "get it." As mentioned earlier, today's young professional family is growing weary of living a duplicitous life. They are seeking respite from the hypocrisy of an integrated Monday through Saturday and a segregated Sunday. Go be a force for change in your church. Don't settle for current reality if it is not consistent with the New Testament mandate for cross-cultural worship. Don't segregate, integrate. An integrated church is an important first step in the journey to cross-cultural worship. However, integration alone is insufficient to drive true cross-cultural worship. Just because different groups come together does not mean the right things will happen. For this reason we must take the second strategic choice.

The second phase of the CCW Model is called "Penetration." Penetration is the process of gaining subsurface insight into the core values and felt needs of people from another racial heritage. The penetration phase builds upon the integration phase. Once people have been brought into physical proximity for the purpose of corporate worship and fellowship, they can benefit greatly from appropriate interaction. An appropriate interaction is one where penetration occurs.

Look again at our definition. You will notice penetration is a process. This phase is where we invest in one another. This is the real stuff of relationships. Think about the one person with whom you have the closest relationship. How long, in a discussion with this person, does it take for you to get beyond the small talk of the day? I am sometimes amazed at what I can share with this person in my life.

Now let me ask the question from a slightly different angle. Think about the one Christian with whom you have the closest relationship. Do you spend most of your time with your closest Christian friend or relative talking about the weather? I hope not. Let me go out on a limb and guess you talk about more than the weather and this morning's newspaper. Perhaps you share important, even intimate things about your life. Maybe this person also shares things about their life. If you are sharing life-impacting matters with another Christian you are experiencing penetration.

Thinking about your closest personal Christian relationship, was it as intimate when you first met as it is today? Most likely the relationship has developed over time and over multiple interactions. By continuing to invest in each other, you have built a relationship typified by deeper knowledge and insight. The two of you over time have learned what is important to the other. You both have developed trust based upon how you have handled the information shared. You have likely found ways to spend time together for sharing and hearing things that matter to you. By doing these things and others you have built a Christian relationship. Hopefully, you pray for one another and study the Word of God together. In this way, the process of penetration takes form and ultimately bears fruit.

Recall, friendship is not enough to drive cross-cultural worship. So the question is what is the difference between friendship and penetration? Friendship occurs when two people invest and confide in each other based upon trust, respect and common interests. You know you have a friend when you begin to confide in the person; you enjoy spending time together; you seek information that helps you support the needs and interests of the other person. Friendship, in any context, is a good thing. It is a very important element of how societies maintain orderly operation and social harmony. Friendship is often a precursor to penetration.

Penetration occurs when two Christians, from different cultural backgrounds, invest in each other's spiritual growth and well-being based upon trust, respect and common interests. You know you have a penetrating cross-cultural relationship when you confide in the person, enjoy spending time together, and seek information that helps you support the other person. With penetration, however, you give and expect to receive a spiritual response to matters tabled for discussion. The beauty of a penetrating relationship is the perspective you receive is often richer and more thought-provoking than you might otherwise receive. The variation in experiences and viewpoints tends to generate more possible remedies. Having more possibilities is really useful when you face a major spiritual or moral challenge in life. A fresh outlook is often energizing when your relationship with God becomes routine and perfunctory.

I have experienced cross-cultural penetration many times over and I cherish deeply those times of mutual investment in each other. Through these relationships, I have grown immensely in my Christian walk. Later, I will share some of the highlights of these experiences in my life.

The scriptural basis for this second phase is found in Colossians 3:9-11 where Paul says, "Lie not to one another, seeing that you have put off the old man with his deeds: and have put on the new man, which is renewed in knowledge after the image of him that created him: where there is neither Greek nor Jew, circumcision nor uncircumcision, Barbarian, Scythian, bond nor free: but Christ is all, and in all." This passage directs us to be honest with our brethren because "honesty is the best policy." We need to be honest with others and with ourselves. Honesty is the principle element in establishing trust. Trust is an essential marker in any true friendship including one of cross-cultural penetration. Paul says we can do this by that new knowledge which is in us. This new knowledge is forged in the example of Christ where there is no difference between Jew and Greek or any other racial affinity group.

Among Christians, according to this passage, it is imperative we learn the value of honest sharing with one another. It is also important we demonstrate such honesty in view of how Christ sees us—as Christians without respect to racial affinities. This is a powerful word of wisdom to each of us in the Church. It speaks directly to the key insight I have found resident in all the penetrating cross-cultural relationships I have enjoyed or witnessed. The insight is "honesty" is what opens the door to the deepest of Christian relationships. This honesty is both in what we say and what we do not say to one another. Often, we share things which are true, but we do not share the things which truly need to be shared.

One reason we do not share what truly needs to be shared is we sometimes find it embarrassing to be personally vulnerable or to probe the sensitive areas of need in others. My observation, which you may find counter-intuitive, is it is often easier to share at this level across cultures than within affinity groupings. This is a very important insight so I want to take a moment and explain how it works.

Within affinity groups there are usually a set of well known social norms, mores and values. These form the rules of engagement in societies where these affinity groups live and work. It matters not where you are from, there are always a set of rules governing interpersonal engagement. By these, we know how to behave and interact socially. The same rules of engagement are naturally extended into relationships formed within the Christian context let's say at Church for example. As you form relationships in Church with others you "bring" these rules with you.

When you are operating within only one affinity group—your own group—everyone in the group will have basically the same rules of engagement. Some things are generally understood even if never stated aloud within the group. I have observed these rules can provide a "limiter" or governor on the depth of exchange and penetration. Since the rules permit the sharing of certain things and preclude others, it is easy for patterns to develop. Conversations tend to go in certain predictable patterns and directions and they often stop short of any real depth or intimacy. Affinity group-based relationships tend to ride along the surface and stay in well-defined comfort zones. Affinity groups rarely go deep unless there is a skilled facilitator to push people beyond these rules of engagement. An Alcoholics Anonymous meeting or a focus group discussion would be good examples of the impact of skilled facilitation. In the Christian context, there is also the rare affinity-based small group (or Sunday School class) which goes beyond the rules of engagement.

However, when a relationship or a small group is formed comprising multiple affinities, each person brings unique rules of engagement to the interaction. One would think this will lead to disharmony and confusion, but I have found interactions tend to go much deeper more quickly than in homogeneous groups. In the cross-cultural groups people are liberated from the constraint of the rules. One person can share something otherwise "out of bounds" because he or she is not expected to know or have in common all the rules of engagement. There is an inherent tolerance which does not exist in the homogeneous interaction. Certain probing questions can be asked which would never find their way into homogeneous group discussion. The power again is in the possibilities. Cross-cultural groups, with blended rules of engagement, will tend to discuss more and deeper topics. Members of these groups tend to allow themselves greater vulnerability because the pressure of living up to a particular set of norms, mores and social values is not constantly in front of them. I will share some examples from actual cross-cultural groups in a later section of the book.

The honesty leads to trust which begets further honesty and generates deeper trust. In this process, the cross-cultural relationship goes deeper and deeper until it reaches a point of radically honest exchange coming from deep within the core values and felt needs of each participant. This going deeper experience is the process of penetration. Do you remember our definition of penetration? Penetration is the process of gaining subsurface insight into the core values and felt needs of people from another racial heritage. Perhaps now you see how this could work in the Church. I tell you, my brothers and sisters it is possible to accelerate penetration through formation of cross-cultural relationships. I have seen and experienced it, and it has changed my life.

So we have seen how the first strategic choice is to integrate the body of believers across racial and other barriers for the purpose of cross-cultural worship. The second choice is to drive penetration among this integrated body of believers. The third and final phase in cross-cultural worship is called "Reconciliation." Reconciliation is a state of Christian symbiosis characterized by high trust level, candid communication and shared leadership. In the largest sense, reconciliation has two key components: reconciliation to God and reconciliation to one another.

The first component of reconciliation is most important—we must be reconciled to God. The scriptural basis for this phase is found in 2 Corinthians 5:17-19. Since we already examined this passage in the beginning of the book, let me only emphasize the extremely important point that God does the reconciling. Paul, in this passage, reminds us "Jesus Christ was in the world reconciling us to God the Father." He also reminds us, as believers, we have been given the ministry and the word of reconciliation. Here is the million dollar question—how are we supposed to execute this ministry of reconciliation? I believe we are to do it via integration and penetration. By bringing people into proximity across the races, and investing to understand and act upon the core values and felt needs of one another, we can set the table for reconciliation to occur.

The biggest learning for me in doing this type of work in churches is the realization God does the reconciling. The passage says, "God has reconciled us to himself by Jesus Christ." We are a new creation in Christ. Our effort in this process is to be busy creating the conditions for reconciliation. We must, through integration and penetration, come together in a meaningful way. By investing in each other as we have been discussing, the preconditions for reconciliation are set. By Jesus Christ each person, regardless of racial or ethnic persuasion, can be reconciled to God the Father. We can be made righteous before God by the power of Jesus Christ.

The second component of reconciliation is also important—we must be reconciled to our fellow man. Though this is desirous for our relationship with all people, it is essential for us within the body of believers. We have already discussed how we are to love our neighbor as ourselves, and we have seen how our neighbor can be those closest to us or furthest from us. This second component of reconciliation assumes our neighbor has been brought together with us to a common place. This common place is the community or the neighborhood. More specifically, it could be the local church where we find expression of our need to worship and fellowship with the saints.

One of the biggest enablers to racial reconciliation among believers is the joint recognition that Jesus is the same Jesus to you as he is to me. The same "saving power" that gave you eternal life is the power that has quickened my spirit to eternal salvation. I have observed that those who struggle with cross-cultural worship tend not to keep in mind the equality of all believers in the economy of Christianity. We were equal in sin before we came to Christ because all who have not received Jesus are bound for hell. Prior to meeting the Lord, we were all seen by God as sinners. The Bible says "All have sinned and come short of the glory of God." I know the world would have us think there are grades of righteousness and that before we were saved, some of us were better off spiritually than others. That simply is not true. The Bible says, "There is none righteous, no not one." The implication of this truth is we were all likewise destined for hell which is eternal separation from God.

Yes, the most effective enabler to cross-cultural worship is to realize spiritually we were all in the same sinking boat—until Jesus rescued our souls from drowning in the tumultuous sea of sin. Now that we are saved from the penalty of such sin, we are still equal. Someone has said, "The ground is level at the foot of the cross" and it is true. However, at the cross we see Christians instituting all manner of inequality. For some reason we feel compelled to find and focus on differences among the brethren. Reconciliation comes when we see each other as fellow servants and joint heirs in the household of faith. In Christ, our relationship is a familial one. In Christ, we are brothers and sisters. In Christ, there are no distant cousins. I am thoroughly convinced if we truly embraced brotherhood and sisterhood in Christ there could be no end to the reconciliation we should expect to see.

Do you remember our definition of reconciliation? It is a state of Christian symbiosis characterized by high trust level, candid communication and shared leadership. Christian symbiosis comes about when we demonstrate we can live together in harmonious and interdependent relationship. The Lord desires this for his Church. The Bible uses the imagery of a body or a vine or even a house to symbolize the unity of the Christian community—the Church. You will notice in each of these analogies we are always referred to as parts of the same whole. We are also always seen as "equal" even though we are not the "same." The Lord has made us different so we can each play distinct parts or roles in the family. This is essential to understand. An issue sometimes arises when we fail to acknowledge the essential nature of ones role or when we try to compare our role to another's role by building ourselves up and denigrating someone else. So symbiosis is an apt word to describe how we should view our relationships within the body of Christ.

I like how the apostle Paul uses the analogy of the human body to describe how the Church should function together. In First Corinthians he proclaims, "The eye cannot say to the hand, 'I don't need you!' And the head cannot say to the feet, 'I don't need you!' On the contrary, those parts of the body that seem to be weaker are indispensable, and the parts that we think are less honorable we treat with special honor. But God has combined the members of the body, and has given greater honor to those that lacked it, so that there should be no division in the body, but that its parts should have equal concern for each other. If one part suffers, every part suffers with it; if one part is honored every part rejoices with it.[31]

This symbiosis, when seen cross-culturally is a most powerful expression of God's desire for us to live and worship together. Some of the indicators of cross-cultural symbiosis are a high trust level, candid communication and shared leadership. As discussed, trust is the key barometer for the health of such relationships: the higher the trust, the better the relationship. Shared leadership is also a key indicator when it comes to cross-cultural worship. Until a group is willing to share leadership, the concept of equality is only a theory or an ideal. When leadership is shared by one group with another, it signifies a crucial step in the development of a group. In a church where leadership is shared, there is a visible expression of equality which speaks to the membership and to any observant onlooker.

When I speak to a church leader about cross-cultural worship, one of the first observations I make is to note the composition of his leadership team. We have seen by just a couple of examples how Jesus and the disciples knew the power and importance of cross-cultural leadership. This is a worthwhile model for us to follow. When shared leadership is not present in a ministry, I often ask why not and what effort has been extended to achieve a diverse Christian leadership team. The answers are always instructive in terms of clarifying the barriers to cross-cultural worship in that body of believers.

The high trust level usually is evidenced by open and candid cross-cultural communication. As we have seen in the discussion of penetration, we are often more likely to see candid and deep exchange when operating cross-culturally. When you see cross-cultural worship activated in a church or small group, it is a powerful sight to behold. This has been my personal experience and we will discuss some examples in the next section.

Implementing the Cross Cultural Worship Model

Now we come to the matter of practical experience. The theory of cross-cultural worship, as expressed in the CCW Model, is very simple. Somehow it seems the work of cross-cultural worship should be more difficult than integration, penetration and reconciliation. Seeing it on paper makes it seem even simpler than when it is articulated verbally. However, whilst it is simple, it can be a challenge to implement. I have seen small groups and even entire congregations established with an integrated composition. In these cases, the groups tend to remain integrated. I have also seen efforts to diversify existing small groups and congregations. In these cases, it can be challenging to overcome the forces of race-based affinity. Sometimes the challenge arises from the membership, but more often the challenge is due to a weak or non-existent desire to integrate by the leadership. You have heard me claim some leaders are out of touch with the pulse of their congregations in gauging potential acceptance of racial reconciliation and cross-cultural worship. This claim is based upon data collected via a tool developed years ago. I still use this tool in my ministry for cross-cultural worship.

Since there are obviously many opinions among believers on the challenge of cross-cultural worship it can be difficult to have a rational and productive discussion on the topic. One enabler to productive discussion is to introduce objective data. To this end I have developed a tool called the Readiness Assessment Survey (RAS).[32] This device uses a few carefully chosen questions to understand a person's readiness for cross-cultural worship. By comparing the data collected from leadership to the data from membership we can see how "in touch" the leaders are with their members. The survey and its findings are very important and useful to understanding the state of readiness for cross-cultural worship. In this section I will explain the survey, provide the biblical basis for each question and share key findings from survey samples already collected.

The survey is comprised of ten binary questions. See the list of questions and their biblical basis.

Q1. Do you think people get along better with each other today than in past years?

Q2. Do you think it is easier for people to accept their differences today than in past years?

Q3. Do you think money makes a bigger difference between people than race?

Q4. Should churches play a bigger role in helping people reconcile their differences?

Q5. Would churches be better off if they encourage people with great differences to join their congregation?

Q6. Do you think parishioners (members) are likely to leave their congregations if different races joined them?

Q7. Do you think people are more likely to express their true feelings to people of other races now than in the past?

Q8. In your opinion will race relations be better in the future?

Q9. Do you feel that you can make a personal difference in reconciling the differences between diverse people?

Q10. From what you know or have heard about Jesus Christ do you think he would be pleased with the present way congregations are formed for worship?

BIBLICAL BASIS FOR READINESS ASSESSMENT SURVEY (RAS)		
Number	Subject	Basis
Q1	Harmony	Romans 12:16-18
Q2	Acceptance	Romans 14:13-19
Q3	Money	James 2:1-10
Q4	Church's Role	2 Corinthians 5:16-21
Q5	Integration	Romans 15:7-12
Q6	Retention	Romans 15:1-6
Q7	Honesty	Colossians 3:9-11
Q8	Hope	Ephesians 2:11-13
Q9	Empowerment	Ephesians 3:7-8
Q10	Pleasing Christ	Acts 2:42-47

The primary purpose of the survey questions is to elicit responses that could be used to measure the potential of the church in general and of individuals in particular to realize cross-cultural worship. Before sharing results of the ten question survey, it is important we understand the basis for each question. Afterward, we will discuss how the questions work together to help give insight into the attitude of the respondent toward cross-cultural worship.

The first question, Q1, is called the "harmony" question. Here we ask do you think people get along better with each other today than in past years. By design, this question is fairly innocuous. It introduces the subject of working with others, but does not speak to race or any other potentially polarizing point of difference. The biblical basis for the harmony question is found in Romans chapter 12 which reads, "Live in harmony with one another; do not be haughty, but associate with the lowly; do not claim to be wiser than you are. Do not repay anyone evil for evil, but take thought for what is noble in the sight of all. If it is possible, so far as it depends on you, live peaceably with all."[33]

The second question, Q2, is called the acceptance question. By asking do you think it is easier for people to accept their differences today than in past years, the survey turns a bit more direct without intruding into any sensitive area. The biblical basis for this question is also seen in Romans when Paul admonished the church to "stop passing judgment on one another." Instead, he says. "Make up your mind not to put any stumbling block or obstacle in your brother's way."[34]

Question 3 or Q3 is called the money question. We ask, do you think money makes a bigger difference between people than race. Here we introduce the twin sensitivities of money and race. It is interesting to note, in my work, I have found money to sometimes be a bigger barrier than race in bringing Christians together. The biblical basis for this question is taken from the Book of James. In chapter 2, the Apostle James says, "My brothers and sisters, do you with your acts of favoritism really believe in our glorious Lord Jesus Christ? For if a person with gold rings and in fine clothes comes into your assembly, and if a person with dirty clothes also comes in, and if you take notice of the one in fine clothes and say, "Have a seat here, please," while to the one who is poor you say, "Stand there" or, "Have a seat at my feet," have you not made distinctions among yourselves, and become judges with evil thoughts?[35]

The fourth question, Q4, is called the Church's role question. Here, we ask should churches play a bigger role in helping people reconcile their differences. This is the first notice the respondent gets that we are doing a "religious" survey. By now they have already warmed up to the idea of discussing sensitive topics. The biblical basis for Q4 is found in 2 Corinthians 5:16-21. We have discussed this passage several times earlier so by now you know the church should play a crucial role in working across differences.

The fifth question, Q5, is called the integration question and comes from Romans 15 where the Apostle Paul says, "Welcome one another, just as Christ has welcomed you."[36] The survey asks would churches be better off if they encourage people with great differences to join their congregations? This question continues with the discussion of what the church should do to work across differences. By using the language of "great differences" after having already introduced the topics of money and race, the respondent is predisposed to answer this question along the same line of thinking. As we have previously discovered, race is often perceived as the greatest difference among people.

Our sixth question, Q6, is called the retention question. The respondent has already shared a point of view respecting integration so we now turn them to the matter of sustainability. Our question is do you think parishioners (members) are likely to leave their congregations if different races joined them. This one cuts to the chase, and drives the respondent to reveal specific attitudes about cross-cultural worship. The scriptural support for this question is also seen in Romans 15. In verses 1-6 we read, "We who are strong ought to put up with the failings of the weak, and not to please ourselves. Each of us must please our neighbor for the good purpose of building up our neighbor. . . May the God of steadfastness and encouragement grant you to live in harmony with one another, in accordance with Jesus Christ."

Question 7 or Q7 is called the honesty question. Here we ask do you think people are more likely to express their true feelings to people of other races now than in the past. In Colossians 3:9-11, we find the biblical basis for this question. The Bible says, "Lie not one to another, seeing that you have put off the old man with his deeds; and have put on the new man, which is renewed in knowledge after the image of him who created him." This question ties to penetration as we probe the perception of how honest people can be in cross-cultural communication.

Question 8 or Q8 is called the hope question. We ask, in your opinion will race relations be better in the future. The scripture basis is from Ephesians 2. In verses 11-13 we read, "Therefore, remember that formerly you who are Gentiles by birth and called 'uncircumcised' by those who call themselves 'the circumcision' (that done in the body by the hands of men)—remember that at that time you were separate from Christ, excluded from citizenship in Israel and foreigners to the covenants of promise, without hope and without God in the world."[37] This question sets up the next question. By asking if things will get better we can direct the respondent to the matter of their role in making things better.

The ninth question, Q9, is the empowerment question. The survey asks do you feel you can make a personal difference in reconciling the differences between diverse people. This question makes it personal and sets up the call to action. Q9 finds its basis in Ephesians chapter 3. Simply put, we seek to follow Paul's example of personal effort given specifically to the task of enabling cross-cultural worship. Paul, in this passage says, "I became a servant of this gospel by the gift of God's grace given me through the working of his power. Although I am less than the least of all God's people, this grace was given me: to preach to the Gentiles the unsearchable riches of Christ."[38]

The final question, Q10, is called the pleasing Christ question. The respondent is asked from what you know or have heard about Jesus Christ, do you think he would be pleased with the present way congregations are formed for worship. This question follows the clear implication of division in the church as expressed in the preceding questions and is answered in light of that implication. The biblical basis for Q10 is found in the second chapter of Acts. Luke offers the beautiful juxtaposition to segregated worship where we read, "They devoted themselves to the apostle's teaching and to the fellowship, to the breaking of bread and to prayer. . .All the believers were together and had everything in common. Selling their possessions and goods, they gave to anyone as he had need. Every day they continued to meet together in the temple courts. They broke bread in their homes and ate together with glad and sincere hearts, praising God and enjoying the favor of all the people. . ."[39]

Just before we examine the survey results let me share more perspective on how the questions work together in five pairings. Despite the brevity of the survey, we can see into the attitudes of each respondent by combining or pairing some of the questions.[40]

KEY PAIRINGS FROM READINESS ASSESSMENT SURVEY

		% Yes				% Yes
Q5	Integration	75	and	Q10	Pleasing Christ	75
Q3	Money	70	and	Q6	Retention	84
Q4	Church's Role	87	and	Q9	Empowerment	83
Q7	Honesty	75	and	Q8	Hope	77

As mentioned earlier, questions 1 and 2 (Q1 and Q2) are designed to get the respondent into the survey without use of polarizing or contentious words or ideas. By asking simple questions like 'do people get along' and 'do people accept differences' the survey sort of eases the respondent into the meatier topics to follow.

The first key pairing is Q5 and Q10. Here we gain insight into the specific attitude toward diversity in the church, that is, cross-cultural worship. Based upon the actual survey results, we observe respondents strongly affirmed (75%) their desire for change by stating, "Churches would be better off if they encourage people with great differences to join" and further acknowledged (75%) their belief Christ would not be pleased with the present way churches are formed for worship. Clearly the implication is for churches to further integrate and to please our Lord by redefining how church congregations are formed for worship. The survey is called a readiness assessment survey, and I think the data from respondents clearly indicates a readiness for cross-cultural worship.

The pairing of Q3 and Q6 provides one of the most important insights from the analysis. Respondents put into perspective the role of "class" in creating division among people. In the "money" question, we ask them to decide if money or race is a bigger issue. Those surveyed strongly affirmed the criticality of status, when 70% said, "money makes a bigger difference than race." In Q6, they support this point by emphatically indicating (84%), "Members are not likely to leave their congregations if different 'races' join them." From this pairing we clearly see money or class can be an even bigger barrier than race. We must keep this in mind when designing strategies for cross-cultural worship.

To some of you, this finding may be counter-intuitive, but for those who grew up in impoverished communities this makes perfect sense. When I was younger, I often wondered how poor White people could turn their noses up at Black people even when the Black people were better off financially. Even when the difference in socio-economic class was obvious or well known, the White folks insisted on maintaining an air of social superiority. The attitude could be described as the lowest class of White person was still above even the highest class of Black person. Of course, this same dynamic sometimes also worked in reverse where Black people held thoughts of superiority. The survey shows the key insight that what people care about is status. My observation is most matters of racial discord in the church carry an implicit class issue alongside them.

The next pairing is of Q4, the church's role with Q9, the empowerment question. Respondents overwhelmingly affirmed (87%) the need for the church to play a bigger role in reconciling the races and clearly felt (83%) personally empowered to make a difference in such reconciliation. This combination indicates not only a desire for change, but asserts that individuals and the church at large should be actively involved in the work of racial reconciliation. I am so encouraged to see this finding because it supports the point that congregants want to see cross-cultural worship made into a reality and they are personally willing to be a part of the solution.

This leads us logically to the last pairing, Q7 and Q8. Respondents offered a strong and positive prognosis for the future of race relations. In the honesty question, 75% of those surveyed said, "people are more likely to express their true feelings to those of other races now than in the past" and 77% insist race relations will be better in the future! This is an encouraging outlook on the future. More than three-fourths of respondents have hope for a better future where races can work together.

When you blend all these pairings you can clearly see the overarching support by those surveyed for the ministry of reconciliation and the mandate for cross-cultural worship. My argument in favor of cross-cultural worship has featured three key elements: the Biblical mandate, empirical demographic trends, and a statistically significant attitudinal survey. By now, perhaps you share my enthusiasm for the New Testament imperative of cross-cultural worship. Maybe you are feeling empowered and hopeful like the survey respondents. I am not sure where you are on this matter, but I hope at this stage you are not in denial.

The RAS survey data is useful for many purposes. I have found the survey effective in helping individuals process their own attitudes about cross-cultural worship and reconciliation between the races. This is best understood by surveying a small sample of respondents and immediately afterward discussing their responses to each question. Often, people will go through a process of self discovery as they learn about their attitudes toward others. Some have later disclosed to me how the survey brought out feelings, even prejudices, they had not considered in some time. The survey also helped to table some of these matters in a context where their thinking could be challenged and sharpened. Of course, I have learned through these individual discussions much more about some of the respondents.

Having surveyed so many people, I can now see the relative comparison of a new respondent to the database of prior survey responses. Occasionally I come across a unique sample and it is intriguing to discuss the survey with such a respondent. It has been very useful to get perspectives from respondents immediately after they take the survey. As mentioned, the individual follow-up discussions are useful, but perhaps more useful is the group survey followed quickly by the group discussion of the survey.

By discussing the survey as a group I find people hear their own opinion reflected in the comments of another respondent. At first, this is reassuring because it gives the person a feeling of validation and acknowledgement. Sometimes, however, when one hears his own opinion articulated by another, he finds it repulsive when uttered aloud. This is the road to growth. Sometimes people within the discussion group will modify their opinion based upon the case made by others. In these cases, I have allowed them to retake the survey. If their responses change, I replace the old sample with their new one, but I retain only one survey per individual in the database.

Perhaps one of the most instructive uses of the survey has been in the context of helping church leadership to understand the attitudes of their congregations. Typically, I will survey a statistically significant sample from within the particular congregation. Before sharing any results with the leadership, I will survey the leadership team. With the leadership team I ask them to complete the survey by sharing how they think the congregation will respond to each survey question. Once all surveys are collected, I compare the leadership responses with the actual congregation sample.

Most often, I find the leadership's projected survey responses do not match the congregation's actual survey responses. Unfortunately, I also find the leadership is usually less optimistic about the readiness of their congregations for cross-cultural worship and racial reconciliation. It is sometimes no wonder why congregations still form along racial lines of distinction when you see the attitudes of the church leadership in this light. Similar to the individual discussions, I often see personal growth in debriefs with leadership using these responses in side-by-side comparison. This tool brings data to a discussion often void of objective insight. I do not have to tell you how important the attitudes of the leadership can be in shaping the attitudes of a congregation. Congregants are looking to their spiritual leaders for guidance in spiritual matters. The good news is my experience has most often led to a series of discussions with these same leaders about how to understand the impact of their personal attitudes and how to reverse the pattern of segregation they see in the churches they pastor. These are the proverbial moments when "iron sharpens iron."[41] These are the moments when I get to play a small part in the development of a local church toward the biblical imperative of cross-cultural worship.

Of course, there are many other uses of the survey, but these few examples give you a feel for the power of the tool in practical application. Since the initial three survey samples, I have continued to collect data using this same survey. I have used the survey in multiple church settings across the U. S. and internationally. It is interesting to note the data continues to converge on the same indications taken from the initial surveys. With thousands now surveyed, I still see extremely high affirmative response rates on the key questions.

THE CROSS-CULTURAL EXPERIENCE

To this point, we have discussed the theory of cross-cultural worship. Whilst this has been a combination of quantitative and qualitative data laced with personal experiences, you may still be wondering how cross-cultural worship works in real life. This is a fair question. The next two chapters address this question by sharing from my experience with three types of cross-cultural small groups and with three different church congregations keen on developing broader and deeper cross-cultural worship settings. These experiences take us from the theoretical to the practical and form additional basis for the principles and approaches offered in this book.

Cross-cultural Small Groups

In this section I will share three very different examples from small groups I have started in varying settings. Each of these small group experiences demonstrated, in different ways, the powerful possibilities available to Christians when we get beyond affinity groups. Through these experiences I have learned the principles of cross-cultural worship hold true in a variety of settings. I will share my experience of starting a small group at my workplace, opening our home to a small group, and beginning a small group Sunday school class on a church campus.

The very first cross-cultural small group I formed was at my workplace in Procter and Gamble's worldwide headquarters located in Cincinnati, Ohio. While working with P&G I attended seminary at the Cincinnati Bible Seminary at Cincinnati Christian University. As mentioned earlier, it was while in seminary I began to really understand the specific nature of my ministry. It was in that time period I realized more fully the challenge and the urgency of cross-cultural worship and fellowship. One of the most enlightening experiences of those early years in this cross-cultural ministry was the formation of a small group comprised of P&G employees.

I started the group as an intentionally cross-cultural effort. We had six men: three Black and three White. I knew each of the men through previous work-related interactions. Knowing each man had a testimony for Christ and an interest in the general issue of racial reconciliation, it made sense for us to connect, discuss, pray and study scripture together. We agreed to meet in the early morning hours before beginning our work day, and for convenience chose to meet in a first-level conference room in the P&G general offices.

From the moment of our first Bible study session this group was an intensely powerful experience for all six of us. As a standard join-up tool, we decided to share our testimonies. I asked, as each man shared, that we include elements of our testimony which speak to the issue of racial reconciliation. I thought we would have an interesting and intellectually stimulating discussion because each of these men is a strong thinker and problem solver. I fully expected it would be a Christ-centered discussion since each of these men is a strong born-again believer with a solid testimony for Christ. What I was totally unprepared for was the incredible experiences each man would share about why they were so intent on seeing racial harmony in the Church. We sat in that small conference room and shared our stories. We became engulfed in the "penetrating realities" of each man's experience. It gripped us, touched us, moved us and has created a bond that will likely never be broken among us. The group is still in touch although more than a decade has passed since we had that initial meeting.

Rather than to recount their stories from memory, I want to share some of the more salient points of their testimonies as they would say it. Even still, some of the effect will be lost since you are not hearing their "live" verbal testimonies. For accuracy, I will quote from their written testimonies recently received in preparation for this book. These five men have had a lasting impact upon my Christian experience. Before sharing their testimonies, let me introduce them and bring perspective and context to their stories of how God has shaped them for cross-cultural ministry.

Kim Robinson, one of the African American brothers in the group, is one of my oldest and closest friends in the company. Kim has been a mentor, confidante, co-laborer and now a peer. Kim is a board member for Focus on the Family and his counsel in many situations of life and work has been invaluable. David Sisk is a Caucasian American whom I have also known for many years. David and I met and served together as unit managers in the Houston, Texas area over twenty years ago. Ken Wilson, an African American, is one who I have been privileged to mentor over a long period now exceeding a decade. Jeff Hirsch worked very closely with me before and during the time this small group was formed. He was and is an amazingly humble man. Eric Admiraal, another Caucasian American, and I met and began working together just a short time before the group was started. These five men and I formed the very first "BASIC" small group.[42] I will always maintain the highest respect and admiration for these men. Their testimonies for Jesus Christ have been strong through many storms of our individual lives. These men also have a burden to see cross-cultural worship in the Lord's Church. Like me, they long to see racial reconciliation in the Church. Perhaps when you hear their stories you will understand why they carry this burden.

In that first meeting, when we formed the group, we shared our testimonies. We laughed and cried and prayed as we sat and listened. It was a special day in each of our lives. Now, let me bring you into that room and permit you to hear some of what we heard that day.

Kim Robinson's story is a good place to begin. He shared a testimony of multi-generational struggle to overcome racism. Here are his words:

> "Between 1882, when reliable data was first collected, and 1968, when the crime had largely disappeared, at least 4730 people in the United States had been lynched. Most of

> the violence, approximately 3440 lynchings, was perpetrated against black men and women. Most of these lynchings occurred in the South during the reconstruction era, when Whites used lynching and other terrorist tactics to intimidate blacks into political and social submission. One of these victims was my great grandfather Clark, who was a successful trading store owner in Mississippi in the early 1900's. Some white citizens in the community were concerned a black man owned and managed his own store. They thought it was a dangerous precedent to be 'fixed.' One day, they decided to drag him from his store, burn it down, and hang him from a tree. Terrified, his family including my grandfather, William Clark, Sr., fled Mississippi and never returned. Although the lynching extinguished a life that shameful day, it also lit a flame in my grandfather's heart to overcome the ravages of racism and excel despite all obstacles."

Hopefully, by now you are already feeling the powerful sense of engagement we all felt that day as testimonies were shared. Kim's story has a tragic beginning. Fortunately, there is more to the story. Kim went on to share how his grandfather would eventually graduate from Tuskegee University with a degree in architecture, which he used to design and build over a dozen "black churches" in Kansas City later in life. As a result of William Clark, Sr.'s perseverance and his determined example, Kim's mother and father were successful in their career endeavors. Their success paved the way for Kim to be a successful executive at P&G. Kim's story is a gripping one, but the best part is to know he gives all the credit to the Lord for the life he now enjoys as an officer in the Procter and Gamble company and the cross-cultural ministry of reconciliation he now so passionately executes.

Next please join me in hearing the testimony of Eric Admiraal. Eric's story is very interesting. To describe his passion for cross-cultural worship and fellowship, Eric shares the following testimony:

> "My dad was pastor of a largely white, Dutch church in Massachusetts in the mid to late 70's. I recall we had a couple of families in the church that were 'different' because they didn't look like the rest of us. The Williams family was a committed, church-going African American family who regularly attended our church. They were the first African Americans I recall coming into contact with . . . and I was five at the time. My parents would often comment about how nice a family the Williams's were and what great believers they were . . . I thought, if they were members of my Dad's church and they liked his preaching, they must be fine people."

Eric's story began with a preacher's kid getting a practical, cross-cultural worship exposure to real people from another racial heritage at a very young age. After hearing Kim's story I admit Eric's is less dramatic; however, it is no less rich with lessons for Christian life. Eric continues,

> "We moved to Kalamazoo, Michigan and lived in a 'mixed' neighborhood with half my neighbors African American, half white. Until I was eight years old, I only had one real experience with anybody who didn't look like me. The first day living in our new house, my sisters went across the street to play with some Black children—also named Williams. After two hours, my sisters came home and said the Williams kids were not allowed to play with white kids. I was stunned!"

Recall, the similar story of Dr. King's youth I shared earlier? This time the Black family cut off a cross-cultural relationship before it really had time to develop. Could they have had the same concerns the white mother had in the King story? I don't know, but it seems to me the idea of avoiding cross-cultural exchange was practiced by many in the early years of civil rights era "integration" in America.

Again, the good news is Eric's story of cross-cultural exposure did not end with the tragic denial of his sisters and their would-be friends from across the street. Eric went on to tell how T. C. Coleman (that is, Terrence Clarence Coleman) and he became the best of friends shortly after the episode with his sisters. For Eric, there was something redemptive in the relationship he had with T. C. and it taught them both about the possibilities friendship affords. By this time in his life Eric knew, "There is something broken in black and white relations . . . but this brokenness does not affect all people."

Eric also related to us how inter-racial marriages brought the reality of race relations closer to home for him. Through one couple, with whom he was friends; Eric saw how the black husband seemed inordinately relaxed and comfortable around his white wife and all their white friends and associates. He would later learn the black guy (also named Eric) did not use race as his lens for finding friends, but sought after those with a common faith. Eric Admiraal's conclusion: faith is stronger than race!

It was not a part of Eric's testimony that long-ago day, but just a few years ago his brother married a black woman. He is the son of a Northern Reformed minister, and she is the daughter of a Southern Baptist minister. Mary and Nate (Eric's brother) met in the Navy while stationed in Japan. They met, in part, because of the common faith which led them to worship in the only protestant church available where they lived and worked.

The Lord has used life experiences to shape Eric into a genuine lover of people. He meets no stranger. He harbors little bias. Years ago, Eric had a professor who wrote a book on the challenge of racial reconciliation in the church. Eric did some of the research for the book and since that time he has been a student of cross-cultural ministry. He was really taken with my research during seminary, and shared it with his wife Karin Admiraal who later wrote an article on me which was featured in the Cincinnati Post.[43]

The next testimony is from Ken Wilson, a very dynamic African American brother who is completely sold out to the ministry and the message of cross-cultural worship. Perhaps a glimpse into his powerful story will grip you as it did all five of us that day in the P&G headquarters. Here are Ken's words:

> "I was born in a 100 percent African American community in Hamilton, Ohio in 1963. I didn't have my first non-Black class-mate until I was in Junior High School . . . My circle of friends were all black, with the exception of a few teammates on my basketball teams . . . Like most young black kids born in the United States during the civil rights era, my parents and grandparents suffered intense discrimination and grave injustice at the hands of white people. My grandfather was hanged by the KKK and left to die, but survived."[44]

Wow! Can you imagine sitting in a room hearing two men recount how their grandfathers were hanged by the neck and left for dead? So many emotions went through my mind when I heard these solemn and gut wrenching accounts. For many, the imagery of such murderous hate crimes as lynching is impersonal. We know of it only as stories of people we do not know. For these men, this hatred knocked at the door of their closest reality. For these men, and now for us, the hatred which gave rise to such murder was brought into ever sharper focus. I could see, in my mind's eye, Kim's great grandfather and Ken's grandfather hanging there suspended between life and death at the hands of their assailants. I could see the torturous reality of how such crimes could initiate a cycle of hatred which has lasted generations. But not only that . . . I could also see through these testimonies the one thing and the one person powerful enough to overcome such profound hatred—the love of Jesus Christ!

The rest of Ken's testimony is a proof text for this type of Christian love. Ken went on to share the story of his father. Remembering the context of our discussion—all of us were P&G employees—the story of Ken's Father was quite poignant. Ken shared, "My dad, as the first black man to work for Procter and Gamble in Cincinnati, often left work to find his car vandalized." We could all immediately internalize the implications of that statement. Personally, I felt the tug of responsibility to help create an increasing sense of community in Cincinnati. Ken took us a bit deeper when he continued:

> "I can remember walking home from basketball practice in the seventh grade from the first integrated school I attended. Every other car that passed would slow down, roll down the window, and call me a 'nigger'. By human nature, we tend to generalize the negative and individualize the positive. Based upon the experience of my loved ones and myself, I developed what I perceived was a legitimate hatred and distrust for white people . . . Anytime I had a choice of where to spend my time and who I wanted to be with, I would choose 100 percent black people.
>
> I started working for P&G in 1988 and struggled badly in my early career. My lack of exposure to that point had not prepared me to successfully operate in a mostly white corporate culture. I floundered . . . until I had a two hour breakfast one day with a man named Bill Blair. I found out we were both Christians and I was transparent with him about my professional struggles in the company. Despite my admission, Bill saw something in me and recruited me to work on his team. Over time, Bill showed how he believed in me, trusted me and loved me. He was the first white person to ever love me. And I loved him back! Because of Bill's love for me I was able to reject the lies and accusations about white people which Satan had filled my mind with over the years. I have committed my life to seeing all people as I believe God sees them."

By now, you see why that long-ago day was such a strong testimony to the power of Jesus Christ. Jesus is able to overcome the forces which divide us. In the Church we need to see the possibilities which come from cross-cultural worship, fellowship and exchange. I thank God for the account of this cross-cultural exchange between Ken and Bill. Because of it, I can see more possibilities for what we—

the Church—can do together. In a similar cross-cultural exchange Kim Robinson came to know the Lord. In Kim's testimony, he shared how Steve Cesler, another Caucasian brother working in P&G, was instrumental in leading him to a saving knowledge of Jesus Christ.

Jeff Hirsch and David Sisk would also share their testimonies. We all sat in that room and marveled at how the Lord had used significant cross-cultural interactions and relationships to shape each man for cross-cultural worship. I also shared a word of testimony, much of which is expounded in this book. After hearing these men praise the Lord through the testimony of their lives, I shared from my experience. I had already come to realize my entire life was really a series of preparatory experiences for the ultimate ministry of cross-cultural worship the Lord would call me to engage.

I recall how my mother, who raised us as a single parent, maintained secular and Christian relationships with people from many types of backgrounds. She knew the importance of cross-cultural exposure for my life. So far back as I can remember there were opportunities for me to know people outside my race. As I mentioned earlier, the power of racial affinity kept me from fully exploring the possibilities of cross-cultural relationships and friendships.

When I was in the fourth grade, my mother decided we would move to a community in Cocoa Beach, Florida so I could attend a school with very high academic standards called Freedom Seven elementary school. I was the only black student and there was only one black teacher. This experience helped me learn how to survive and later thrive in an all-white environment. Throughout my school years, I would have hundreds of teachable moments including those already mentioned from the fifth, seventh and tenth grades. I have been blessed to experience so many types of combinations of people groups including all black affinity groups, bi-racial and multi-racial mixed groups inside and outside the Christian church.

However, as I shared my testimony with those five men, it was the history of my maternal heritage which was emphasized. You see I am the grandson of a black preacher—Reverend Andrew Witherspoon. My grandfather preached through a mostly itinerant ministry in middle Tennessee and southern Kentucky. Though my grandfather died one year and one month before I was born, he had a profound and lasting impact upon my life. Through the stories of his life I have learned so much.

My grandfather's father also called Andrew was a slave. His story provides the foundation of cross-cultural interaction and relationships in my family. He was not hanged like we saw in the stories of Kim and Ken. However, he could well have suffered a similar torture for what he did. It seems he fell in love with the slaveholder's daughter! My great grandfather had a skill with horses. He was able to teach them to do unique cadences when they would walk. This was so specific a technique; you could identify one of his horses, while the horse was pulling a carriage, even if you could not see the horse. You could identify the horse by the unique sound of his gait.

Because of his skill and otherwise very calm disposition, my great grandfather was privileged to leave the plantation at times. Andrew or "Pap" as they called him, would later elope with my great grandmother, Liza, while on a supposed road trip to another plantation. They married and later settled down to start a family. From their progeny came my grandfather; from him came my mother and me. I shared this and more on that day with my five brothers in that small conference room.

Well, I am certain you can see that day was a real watershed moment in my life. The memory of those testimonial stories has left an indelible impression upon the printed canvass of my life. I will always appreciate the incredible transparency each man showed that day and growth we all experienced from those early moments altogether in that small conference room.

From that initial meeting, we went deeper and deeper with each other. We met each week at the appointed time, and we enjoyed a high quality of fellowship and study of the Word of God. Our Bible study sessions were rich with insights and wide open sharing. It seemed we engaged the scripture in the most personal of ways; yet we did so openly with each other. I sometimes felt the things we shared were like the rare treasures of our personal lives.

After we had solidified our inter-relationships through studying the Bible and sharing our lives, we began to meet outside the study time. We would eventually get our families together and progress in fellowship like any other Bible study group who was together for a while. However, there was a key difference. We had experienced together a true cross-cultural "penetration" each with the other. We had gained subsurface insights into each other's core values and felt needs. We had engaged, actively and specifically, in the work and ministry of reconciliation.

Each of us is still somehow involved in that same ministry which we practiced together long ago. Time and change has created physical distance between us, but we have not been separated from the common work God called us each to do. As I was preparing to write this section, I realized I had not spoken to a couple of the men in quite some time. I sent a single e-mail to all five guys at once. Almost instantly, I received replies from everyone. With those replies, I felt the wonderful experience of our small group flooding back into my remembrance. A smile the size of a rainbow came over my face and the joy of our common experience invaded my mind.

I thank the Lord for that small group Bible study with my colleagues. It had a profound impact upon my outlook toward cross-cultural worship. The Lord used these five men and their families to teach me many things. Looking back, I now see how the Lord would continue at each point to grow my experience in cross-cultural fellowship; to expand my insights and knowledge of cross-cultural reconciliation; and open my mind to the endless possibilities emerging from cross-cultural worship. From this, my very first cross-cultural small group, I draw deep learning and growth points.

The next small group experience is from an in-home group my wife Karen and I started in our home in Springdale, Arkansas. The group was also called "BASIC" or Brothers and Sisters in Christ. Again, we experienced the radical possibilities for penetrating spiritual relationships available when we get beyond race-based affinity groups. Like the first group, we started with members from multiple racial backgrounds. We handed out flyers in the neighborhood and started the group on an agreed kick-off date. Unlike the first group, we began this second group mostly with couples. We also had a few single folks who were studying at the University of Arkansas.

The group was fantastically and refreshingly transparent very early after the start-up. Karen and I began to realize the power of the cross-cultural composition of the group in quickly getting past the surface interactions. After only a couple sessions we were amazed at how deep the group had gone with its sharing.

Some of the most powerful exchanges in this small group were generated by Kimberly and Curtis, a young African American couple who we met in Church. Curtis was a graduate student at the University of Arkansas and Kimberly was an executive with a local bank. Kimberly was so honest and open-minded in her communication; it had an infectious impact upon the rest of the group.

I recall, one exchange where we discussed attitudes we had toward other races. Normally, such a discussion would go through a protracted series of niceties. Everyone would share how they "loved everybody" and how some of their best friends were from other races. The conversation would then go through various twists and turns of surface interactions designed to demonstrate how "tolerant" we each were in relating to people with great differences. It would only be after hours of investment that someone would break down and offer a statement of limited vulnerability which would change the course of discussion. After hours someone might choose to share a momentary breach in their otherwise perfect history of working across races. Then, and only then, we would be able to get past the dainty little stories of perfect past encounters which typified our lives. Without having to say it, I believe we all expected this discussion to be like those I have just described. Perhaps this discussion would also have followed the same pattern. But Kimberly would take us on a different course altogether.

When I set up the discussion, by sharing the Bible passage we would study and giving a brief ice breaker, Kimberly was first to speak. Her opening words were, "I hated white people." Everyone was politely shocked, not appalled, just shocked! Then she proceeded to share how her life had been changed by positive cross-cultural interactions both inside and outside the Church. Kimberly's disclosure set us on a very different course of discussion. It was a much more candid course. If any of us had inhibitions, they were immediately tossed out of the window. We were at once freed from the predictable pattern and each person shared in a fresh, vigorous discussion. From that point forward, we would enjoy one of the most open and brutally honest small group environments I have ever witnessed.

Our discussions of the Bible were at a depth and breadth so powerful, we all could hardly wait for Thursday evening to roll around each week. We never had to call and remind the small group members to come to the discussions. People would often come early and stay late. My wife Karen and I would be amazed at how these small group discussions would go for hours on end. In the late evening when the group discussion would end and members would go home, we would sit and talk for another hour or more.

The Lord blessed us through each weekly discussion. We learned many lessons for how to enable cross-cultural worship. We laughed and cried and grew so much through this small group experience. One of the more senior couples, Joe and Shirlene, shared how much the class opened their outlook to the merit of cross-cultural worship. It was always a joy to watch Joe and Shirlene interact with Curtis and Kimberly. Their backgrounds were like polar opposites. The young African-American couple grew up in the east and were at a life stage when more adventure was ahead than behind. The elder couple was a southern gentleman and a gracious southern belle who had raised grown children and served a lifetime in the church. In a natural sense they could not be further apart. However, we all learned through this small in-home group just how much they had in common as Christians. These two couples would be members of another cross-cultural small group we started in a local church in Northwest Arkansas.

To facilitate discussion in this group we studied many of the New Testament passages which speak to the challenge of cross-cultural worship and fellowship. We studied through the book of Ephesians and at each study time saw ourselves grow deeper and deeper. We applied the truth of how the Apostle Paul and the first-century church addressed the challenges of living out faith in Christ with those from very different backgrounds. The applications were rich with meaningful and candid sharing of the journeys each person had taken in learning to work across cultures. Each week was powerfully engaging.

When we would study passages like Ephesians 2:13 which states, "But you who were afar off have been made nigh (or near) by the blood of Christ" we would see the Gentile's new relationship of brotherhood with the Jewish believers. We would see how Christ broke down the middle wall of partition between these two groups by his death on the cross. In those same discussions, we would see how that same Christ broke down the walls of segregation in our own land. We would share what it meant for each of us to share a cross-cultural brotherhood in Christ in this day and in this age.

Weekly we learned how the blood of Christ was always designed to bring people together across prior lines of separation. Ephesians 3 describes how God once hid the truth of how Gentiles were fellow heirs and partakers of the same promise as the Jews, but now has fully revealed it for all to see. Similarly, the American Church now has to be reminded we are fellow heirs and partakers of one promise in Christ. In this class, we often seemed to unearth new ways of understanding the practical reality of being fellow heirs. Somehow, in America, Black men and White men got the idea their inheritance was different. Somewhere we got the idea the graces of our Lord and the power of His Spirit fell uniquely upon only "some" of the brethren. Each week we ripped apart this type of thinking through cross-cultural penetration experienced in the context of serious Bible study.

The third small group experience I will share is from a group Karen and I started in a local church setting in Northwest Arkansas. Perhaps more than any other small group we have started, this one taught us the power of cross-cultural worship and fellowship in

Jesus Christ. Perhaps, after hearing the stories of my two earlier examples, you may be thinking what could make this group Bible study even more powerful.

It has been said, "The Lord works in mysterious ways." Well, I believe he does. This third group was a constant reinforcement of how God can move in the lives of his people as he blesses the works of their hearts in fellowship; the works of their heads in Bible study; and the works of their hands in community service. Each week we saw the blessings of God fall fresh upon us, but before I give you some of the details of our experience let me tell you a bit about this group. Though it was built upon the same premise as the first two small group examples, it had a few distinctive characteristics.

The group was also called BASIC, an acronym for Brothers and Sisters in Christ. Contextually, it was not really a small group—it was a Sunday school class. We met on the campus of the First Baptist Church of Springdale, Arkansas where Karen and I were members. First Baptist was, and still is, a vibrant ministry in Northwest Arkansas. The senior pastor, Dr. Ronnie Floyd and I developed a strong relationship from the moment we were introduced by Rev. Drew Tucker, a fellow preacher who was on staff at First Baptist. As Ronnie and I shared our hearts for the ministry, we connected on the challenge of cross-cultural worship. From the moment of our introduction we continually shared ideas about how to do "the ministry of reconciliation" in our context there in Arkansas.

One outgrowth of these ideations was the establishment of the BASIC class. Have you ever been part of something which simply felt right and good? My experience in this particular Sunday school class was such a thing. Every time the class met it seems the Lord confirmed the power and potential of our experience together. Each class session was enriching in so many ways: I felt challenged, supported, loved, respected and closer to God than ever before. And I sensed many in the group felt the same. Though this class no longer meets formally, a number of us maintain contact and enjoy the lasting impact of our experience years ago. It is like the feeling one gets from being part of a very close-knit family.

As I reflect on the experience it is easy for a flood of recollections to rush into my mind, but let me share just a few of those memories. Though I will not take time to share the whole story of this class, I hope you see the unusually high quality of engagement we saw every time we met to study God's Word.

Right from the start, we established that this class would be cross-cultural in composition. Given our context, this was worth mentioning overtly. We were in a part of Arkansas once famous for its effort to maintain racial segregation. I also shared our intent to utilize the power of our racial and social diversity to draw deeper insights into the Bible. This was an exciting thought for most in the class. However, since we started the class from a pre-existing Sunday school group, some did not share our excitement. They were hoping for a continuation of what they had known with the previous teacher and they were not interested in our vision for this Bible study. The class size initially dropped from a start-up group of just over twenty participants to just under fifteen regular attendees who stuck with us for the long haul.

Several members of the in-home small group now also attended our new Sunday school class. Once the class size settled down it all began to take root. The discussions were just as deep and penetrating as what we had experienced with the in-home group. I was pleasantly surprised to see how members would bring visitors to the class each week. I was also impressed with how despite a constantly evolving class composition the level of engagement never waned. Even the first-time visitors would jump right into the sharing. It was a contagious engagement which persisted for years.

The same direct and brutally honest discussion style was evident. We were seeing in Sunday school a mirroring of the honest and rigorous sharing we came to appreciate with all our previous BASIC small groups. This new class not only took root, but it soon began to grow like a weed. Eventually, we had over one hundred members in the class. Yet, the level of sharing remained so in-depth and intense. In fact, it went even deeper than what we had previously experienced with other small groups.

So why was this class inclined toward such a high quality of sharing? What were the common elements in these three examples which led to such quality? One common element was that I led each of the groups. Perhaps it was something about the way I prepared the lessons or the style with which I taught. Frankly, I don't think this was the key ingredient that led to our effectiveness. I think it was much more than my personal presence or ability. Do you want to know what I think was the real force behind the quality of these Bible study experiences? Glad you asked.

I think the real force behind these groups was the Lord. I think the Lord honored our effort to execute the Biblical imperative of cross-cultural worship. We got so close because God brought us together—integration. We went so deep because God took us beneath the surface—penetration. And many of us are still in touch with one another because God has linked us together as brothers and sisters in Christ—reconciliation.

Each week, when the class would meet, I would have to gather all my energy to teach the class. I never knew what would happen in class, but I always knew something big would happen in class. One day an attendee shared a powerful prayer request and a testimony of how she had personally grown in relating to Christians from different backgrounds. By the way, the prayer requests were often displays of extraordinary transparency and trust. Well this prayer request captured our full attention. Another attendee—Delesslyn Kennebrew—was so moved by the prayer request she broke out in an impromptu song. The song was so beautifully sung. It was so sincere and genuine that when she finished singing there was hardly a dry eye in the room. I almost passed the offering plate and gave an invitation to discipleship! Normally, in my experience, when a class meets and shares prayer requests and testimonies, it can be a bit of a surface exercise. In this class, there were rarely any surface exchanges. People spoke so freely it was like reading from an open book—the open book of their lives.

On another occasion, a member of the class shared how her husband had been diagnosed with cancer and asked, according to James

5:14, for a prayer of healing. When the class met the following Sunday, we prayed for them and anointed him with oil in the name of the Lord according to scripture. Though God does not choose to heal every person who receives such a prayer, our class experienced the joy of this person's eventual healing. Again, when he later shared his testimony of healing and we learned the cancer was in complete remission, there was hardly a dry eye in the room.

It is true we were sometimes moved to tears in this class. However, it was a class that often burst out in hearty laughter. Once we were considering a Bible passage where a crowd of people just took off running. To illustrate the point I shared how the Bible characters reminded me of my African American upbringing. I implied there could easily have been some Black folks in the crowd. My logic was based upon the observation that when a potentially dangerous situation is unfolding, black folks can sometimes take off running without hesitation. Caucasians, on the other hand, might stand around asking questions like, "What's going on"? Black folks don't need to know what is happening, they just know it is time to get moving. When I shared this illustration the entire class erupted into laughter. This is a simple example of using the differences in our cultural experiences to illuminate the Bible.

By drawing such contrasts in a proper context we saw the gradual release of various forms of cross-cultural relational baggage and bias we all seemed to carry. We witnessed an increasing willingness to let go of the effort we would normally expend to protect our racial and ethnic affinity-based experiences. We no longer seemed to need the exclusivity of racial affinity; instead, we saw person after person going beyond their prior bias and investing across racial and ethnic boundaries. We were doing the ministry of reconciliation!

Perhaps more important than crying and laughing, we learned quite a lot while studying the Word of God together. By bringing such divergent perspectives together we challenged so many previously uncontested paradigms. People read the study passages between classes. They came prepared to engage the material. As a teacher I learned so much and we all grew in the knowledge of the Lord.

When we engaged a passage of scripture the richness of varied experience came out in robust discussion. When someone disagreed, they said so. When disagreement was voiced, instead of shutting down, people opened up even more. Because we had a variety of ages represented we had different levels of personal experience in walking with the Lord. Older Christians shared their perspectives and younger Christians listened intently. When the younger members offered their thoughts they were often affirmed by older members. The mutual respect was poetic.

We were doing the ministry of reconciliation. We were constantly penetrating beneath the surface with one another. We were constantly living out a willingness to think and share and work across cultural barriers. Eventually, such penetration was second nature. No one had to think about it. We just did it!

The group not only grew larger, it grew stronger. Once we felt and saw evidence of the spiritual growth of so many class-mates, we eventually turned our attention outward. The class undertook service projects in the community together. One of our big projects was to restore a Christ-centered facility for women and children who were victims of abuse and abandonment. We painted, replaced carpet, repaired ceilings and replaced furniture. When Christmas came, we bought all the presents for the families and spent Christmas day with these mothers and children exchanging gifts and hugs. We all had a meal together and nearly half our class showed up to help with the work and celebrate the birth of our Lord. Of course people in our class grew closer through these shared experiences.

This small group was highly functional. We had a healthy engagement during and outside the class sessions. As a teacher and leader of the class, I was often amazed at how the people would embrace new thinking or offer opposing views with tremendous transparency. I have been part of many small groups and Sunday school classes. I have had oversight for scores more classes than I have personally attended. Of all the small groups I have known this one had the most profound effect upon my understanding of cross-cultural worship, study and fellowship.

In fact, all three of these small groups contributed to my current understanding of cross-cultural worship. Hopefully, by seeing some of the highlights of these experiences you are beginning to see connections between the theory and the practice of working across cultural barriers to advance the cause of Christ. As I noted earlier, the practical examples will be in small group and local church examples.

We begin the discussion with the small groups because in some ways it is an easier task to drive cross-cultural penetration in small groups versus whole congregations. The primary benefit of the small group setting is its "smallness." Intimacy, transparency and depth of discussion are more readily achieved in smaller groups. In general, trust is often higher within small groups because it is a safer environment. When there are fewer participants in something, there is higher personal accountability in driving mutually agreed outcomes. For example, if a participant makes a confidential disclosure and this is shared outside the group it is easier to isolate the one who broke the confidence of the group. Over time participants have a shared history of discussion. This common historical perspective often provides important context for current discussion. Yes, smaller groups have natural advantages in facilitating cross-cultural engagement. However, cross-cultural worship can be effectively advanced with whole congregations. And this is true across churches of different locations and of varying sizes.

Cross-cultural Worship in the Local Church

It has been my privilege to work with Pastoral staff teams in numerous churches to help bring cross-cultural worship to life. I am a big believer in the criticality of the local church setting as a primary venue for spiritual development. So it makes sense to marry up what we now know about the biblical model of cross-cultural worship with real church experience. I want to share three of those church experiences.

The first church is Forestville Baptist in the Cincinnati, Ohio area. It was here the Lord first made known to me the full importance of cross-cultural worship and racial reconciliation in the Church. It was this church where many of the concepts in this book were formulated and applied for the first time.

The second church is First Baptist in Springdale, Arkansas. This ministry represented a very different challenge from the Forestville experience. Forestville was an average sized church with under five hundred members, but First Baptist Springdale was a mega-church with over ten thousand members. At Springdale, the Lord brought even greater clarity to the principles and practices which best enable genuine cross-cultural worship.

The third church is International Baptist Church of Singapore. Yes I said Singapore—the tiny Southeast Asian island nation located just off the southern coast of the Malaysian peninsula. This is a unique church congregation with over forty five nationalities represented each week in corporate worship services. The Lord has used this particular church experience to more completely solidify in my mind the principles and practices of cross-cultural worship.

Maybe the best way to share the insights from these three church settings is to tell the stories of our work within each of these congregations. The three stories build one upon another. The "Forestville" story lays a foundation for understanding the imperative and urgent nature of the need for cross-cultural worship. The "Springdale" story takes the foundational truths into a larger, more complex setting. Finally, the "International" story exposes whole new dimensions of the cross-cultural mandate.

The Forestville Story

Forestville Baptist Church is situated in a suburban setting on the east side of Cincinnati, Ohio. The Forestville story begins with a conscious decision my wife and I made years before moving to Cincinnati. We decided to worship in the community where we lived. Now, as a young couple with very young children we found ourselves in a new city—Cincinnati—with new possibilities. We chose to live in a part of the city with good property value appreciation and a top-rated school district. In this location we saw the opportunity for a safe environment due to relatively low crime rates, and convenient access to all types of services and facilities important to young families.

These possibilities were very encouraging. However, they did not come without trade-offs. By choosing this neighborhood, we would not have proximity to what we call "the hood" or the neighborhoods where larger groups of African Americans chose to live. Karen and I had both spent most of our youth in predominately African American working class neighborhoods. We grew up with an appreciation for the strong sense of community we experienced as part of what is clearly a "common black experience." Even today, this experience can be readily tapped as a source of commonality among African Americans whom we meet all over the world. There is a certain comfort which comes with the familiar. But we had chosen the less familiar. We chose a neighborhood, not on the basis of familiarity and a common past, but on the basis of possibilities and a different future.

This was not the first time we had made such a choice. Since we were married, we had never really lived in the type of neighborhoods where we grew up. When we were married we made two key decisions about where we lived. First, we decided not to use racial composition as a determinant in housing selection. Second, and perhaps more important, we decided to worship in the community where we lived. This is significant, as we would later discover, because many African Americans in our same demographic profile would choose to live in one community, but drive across town to worship in an altogether different community. Indeed, many chose to live in suburban communities, but worship in the hood.

We lived only a few minutes from Forestville Baptist Church, located in Anderson Township on Cincinnati's east side. It would be an understatement to call this area predominately Caucasian. Nearly ninety-nine percent of the Anderson residents were Caucasian, according to data from the 1990 U. S. Census Bureau report and the 1997 updates to that report. We could go days without seeing people of color in our neighborhood. Sometimes we got the distinct impression our "neighbors" were surprised to see us there. At times we felt like strangers in our own neighborhood. It was sometimes not a very comfortable experience.

I don't have to tell you the United States is still suffering in the wake of its deep and pervasive racial disunity. Sometimes, when we move "up" the socio-economic ladder we can become divorced from the reality of modern-day segregation and disunity. I call it the "scratch and sniff" principle. Let me explain.

As a nation, America has become increasingly affluent as indicated by continuously rising annual household income, now at $66,570 on average. Yes, Americans are enjoying greater financial wealth and this is reflected in rising consumer spending. Of course, African Americans are part of this shift in affluence. Median annual household income for Black families is $45,127—the highest in U.S. history. However, African American households earn less than Caucasian, Asian or Hispanic American households who earn $71,745, $88,293 and $50,575, respectively.[45]

Despite obvious disparity in average household income between racial groups in America, there are more wealthy African Americans than any prior point in American history; and economic opportunity in America has produced thousands of Black millionaires and even billionaires—such as Oprah Winfrey. While Caucasian Americans now comprise less than fifty percent of U. S. population, Caucasian households comprise more than ninety percent of the 2.2 million U. S. households earning more than $250,000 per year.[46] Still this leaves minorities with over a quarter million U. S households earning annual incomes of at least $250,000. If you divide the U. S. population into quintiles, the top quintile of about 23 million households would each earn just under $100,000 per annum. These families, like their more wealthy counterparts, are choosing to live in communities commensurate with their financial means. It is, therefore, becoming more difficult to segregate communities by simply raising the cost of housing and services. Hence, even the wealthiest neighborhoods are becoming increasingly integrated.

Earlier, we proved the demographic reality that people are migrating to the larger urban areas, and this is creating greater racial and ethnic diversity in those cities. Now we see, within the cities, the communities are diversifying too because the wealth, however slowly, is being distributed among the various racial groups. So what does this have to do with our experience in Anderson Township?

Well, this community was one of well above average affluence. Admittedly, it was a bit naïve, looking back, but I thought if we could afford to live in this community we would be accepted as neighbors. I was a young executive at Procter and Gamble, the largest purveyor of consumer goods in the world and living in the headquarter city of my company. We had the means to live in that community. Our expectations were high; and as I said earlier, we were looking for possibilities. After all, I had always been taught both economic opportunity and access to education were key to social acceptance, even social equality. Our prior experiences of working and living with various types of people prepared us to live anywhere we chose. We were ready to live in Anderson Township. But Anderson Township was not ready to live with us!

This low crime area seemed peaceful and calm. When we first arrived we drove around and checked out all the facilities so nicely tailored for families. The first few Sunday mornings we went searching for a place to worship. The churches were not at all inviting. They were somewhat cordial, but clearly uncomfortable with our presence. This went on for several weeks. One Sunday, following a similar experience, we went to lunch at a local restaurant chain. We entered the restaurant in the middle of the after church rush period. The place was packed and a quick scan upon entry revealed it was a bit of an older crowd. As the hostess came to seat us, and the patrons noticed our presence, the noisy crowd fell into a hush of deafening silence. It had been some years since I felt the coldness of that Sunday afternoon lunch reception.

We chose not to eat in that restaurant. As time passed, we would experience more coldness. When our furniture arrived and we moved into our home, a neighbor brought over a fresh-baked loaf of "monkey" bread and rang the doorbell. I love monkey bread![47] We were busy unpacking, so my wife answered the door in an apron and with a scarf tied around her hair. When Karen answered the door our neighbor asked, "Is the lady of the house home"? Karen answered, "I am the lady of the house." Astonished, the neighbor said, "No, I mean the owner of the house." Disappointed, Karen had to explain we were the intended recipients of the monkey bread. Such insults, unfortunately, were not infrequent. Even our children, though small and innocent, would hear the "N-word" yelled, among other expletives, at our family while driving in this, our new community.

It occurred to us, in those early days of residency in Anderson Township that something was afoul. This seemingly tranquil community with its low crime rate and its family-centric facilities and its appreciating real estate was suddenly not the place of possibilities we had hoped. To the casual observer, all was calm and peaceful and lovely here. But to a young, enthusiastic Black family it was not all it was cracked up to be. It was like we had seen the less pleasant side of "Pleasantville."

Years ago, it became common to receive samples in the mail of scented products. Sometimes they were perfumes or dish washing liquids or other products where the scent is a crucial selling point. A new technology enabled the scent to be captured between a lightweight paper stock and a surface film. The advertising copy was printed on the paper with an invitation to "scratch and sniff." When you would scratch the film off the paper the fragrance would be released. In an instant, the would-be buyer was sampled on the new product—at a much lower cost than sampling trial size packages of the actual product.

When we scratched the surface film off the canvass of our new community we discovered the odiferous stench of racial prejudice. I call this the scratch and sniff principle because it seemed normal on the surface, but just beneath that surface was the reality of racism. Below the veneer of hospitality was a pinned up hostility. It seems we had somehow scratched the surface and released what lay beneath.

However, things were different in one tiny place in Anderson Township—the church at Forestville Baptist. We joined Forestville because the people seemed to care for us before we even joined the congregation. The senior pastor at the time, Dr. David Price, came to visit us while my wife was in the hospital. We met when Karen and I visited Forestville for the first time. He hardly knew us—we had only visited the church once before—but invested nine hours waiting with me during Karen's complicated surgery. We developed a lasting relationship and I eventually would enjoy the full support of this church throughout my time in seminary and our entire stay in the Cincinnati area. I was licensed and ordained to preach the gospel in this church. You see, sometimes the Lord has a plan for our lives which goes well beneath the surface of what we can see. Sometimes, if we would endure the present God prepares for us a brighter future.

As close as I was with Dr. Price I was even closer to then youth pastor, Rev. Brent Jones. Brent and I would spend countless hours discussing the ministry and challenging the contradiction we both saw in segregated worship services. All those extended conversations with Pastor Brent helped to sharpen my early thinking on the challenge of cross-cultural worship. Now, a decade later, we still engage to share our experiences and dream together for true cross-cultural worship and fellowship among the people of God.

Earlier in this book, I described the readiness assessment survey (RAS) which I developed for a seminary project. The survey was first administered in Anderson Township. We surveyed Christians and non-Christians in church settings and in public areas alike. Among Christians we found a clear affirmation of the Church's role as an enabler to racial reconciliation and cross-cultural worship. We also found non-Christians shared the same view in their response to Q4—do you think churches should play a bigger role in helping people reconcile their differences? My conclusion was people in Anderson Township, whether Christian or not, and despite all the pinned up prejudice, could see the need for the Church to play a bigger role in reconciliation. This insight, coupled with other data from the survey, formed the basis of a decision by the Forestville leadership—advisory board and deacon council—to take positive action toward cross-cultural worship.

Given our experience in this community, you might imagine my surprise when I learned God was calling me to an active ministry of racial reconciliation in this community. This was my Ninevah! This was hardly the place where a Black preacher was likely to feel a warm reception. Like Jonah, I had developed a point of view I could be more useful elsewhere. Unlike the Prophet Jonah I was brief in my resistance to the Lord's calling. I believe most preachers have a Ninevah. Anderson Township had become mine, but God's grace was kindled in my heart. While in seminary, God began to help open my eyes to the true reason we had moved to this community. He began to reveal to me, once again, the possibilities of this new community.

I developed the initial work for what is now the Cross Cultural Worship Model and called it the "Forestville Reconciliation Model." I still recall the night I presented this concept to the advisory board and the deacons of Forestville. The early evening meeting was supposed to last two hours. Instead, we discussed the possibilities of cross-cultural worship and the opportunity for Forestville to be a force in racial reconciliation until after midnight.

I had never seen that group of men so engaged in any ministry decision, but the vision was evident. A few of the brothers initially objected. They saw the limitations. Rooted in historical perspective, they were concerned it may not work. I was not deterred. I remembered the words of Jesus in Luke chapter 9, "No man, having put his hand to the plow and looking back, is fit for the kingdom of God." I had gripped the plow of reconciliation and I would not look back. That night it was agreed Forestville would embrace the ministry of reconciliation. It was also agreed pastor Brent Jones and I would co-lead this effort. The church set me aside to this work and we did the work of reconciliation. Reverend Brent Jones is now senior pastor at Forestville. He and many members of Forestville are forever joined together with us in the bond of peace and the brotherhood of love.[48]

Those early years at Forestville Baptist Church were foundational to all Karen and I now know about cross-cultural worship, Bible study and fellowship. While worshipping there, we enjoyed a sweet fellowship with believers. We shared and continue to share deep and abiding cross-cultural relationships formed with our brothers and sisters there.

So if things were so great for us at Forestville, you may ask what happened to the composition of the congregation and what impact did the church have on the surrounding community? These are fair questions. When we first joined Forestville, we were the church's only minority family. There were also two inter-racial couples. By the time we left, minorities comprised nearly seven percent of the congregation. The community also developed into a less homogeneous composition. We had accurately predicted the shifting demographic trends would eventually bring more integration to this historically White neighborhood. Recently I was there and the optics of Anderson Township are clearly evolving. When we lived there one could go days without seeing minority families in the shops and restaurants around town. Now it is impossible to miss the obvious ethnic and racial diversity in Anderson Township.

Pastor Brent still has the same dream to see Forestville become a place known for cross-cultural worship and fellowship. In a recent conversation, he shared with me how the church is enjoying added ethnic and racial diversity. They are experiencing the first phase of cross-cultural worship—integration. As the surrounding community becomes more diverse, Forestville is positioning itself as a place where all are welcome to experience the love of Christ and to enjoy the blessing of cross-cultural worship, Bible study and fellowship.

The Springdale Story

First Baptist Church of Springdale, Arkansas is in a very different setting from Forestville Baptist. Pastor Ronnie Floyd is leading a major ministry in a mega-church setting across multiple campuses. The Northwest Arkansas-based ministry serves our Lord and ministers to thousands every week of the year. Again, this is a very different setting from the Forestville Baptist Church setting where the church served the Lord with an above average size congregation of about two hundred families.

The challenge at Springdale was to understand the role of cross-cultural worship in an external context of historical segregation and in a ministry already experiencing rapid growth. Pastor Floyd and I spent hours discussing this very challenge. What was evident to me, through those discussions, was his heart for the ministry, his desire to make a profound impact for the cause of Christ, and his evident appreciation for the Biblical mandate of cross-cultural worship.

In our very first meeting, we discussed cross-cultural worship and the Church's role in racial reconciliation. We concluded there was, in fact, an opportunity to do the work and the ministry of reconciliation at Springdale. I agreed to develop a strategy to later share with Dr. Floyd and key members of the Springdale staff.

The strategy was to move without fanfare. I worked behind the scenes to assess the situation and develop a formal plan including the in-home and Sunday school small groups previously discussed. In the year 2000, we began to slowly develop and Implement the plans for cross-cultural worship in Springdale. In January I developed a document entitled "Reconciliation Strategy for First Baptist Church of Springdale" and shared it with Pastor Floyd. This document laid out an approach including key principles, strategic framework and several tactics suggested for immediate action.

Within two weeks we were already moving into action with the critical first step of assessing the church environment. The assessment included four key components: external and internal demographics and external and internal readiness insights. The readiness insights were a combination of the RAS or readiness assessment survey tool described earlier and direct interviews of key leaders and congregants from across the strategic growth areas in the ministry.

Our learning was robust from the assessment phase. We spent seven months from February 15 to mid September collecting the data from a broad cross section of the ministry. I personally interviewed the key leaders of the church and especially those leading the growth areas within the ministry (e.g., young married couples, youth, missions, small groups, etc.). These interviews gave me an appreciation for the collective interest in cross-cultural ministry held by many among the key leadership. Some of their stories were amazing as it relates to cross-cultural experience. It was also quite instructive to note how few among these key leaders had active and important cross-cultural relationships.

An important component of my work with the leadership was to survey them using the RAS tool. As part of the assessment, I examined the comparison of responses taken from the leadership with those of the broader church membership and my larger database of survey respondents. On several points there were statistically significant differences between the Springdale staff responses and those of the congregation and base benchmarks and these became specific components of the strategy going forward. The strategies, initially outlined in January, were now expanded and refined. I prepared a formal summary of the findings and released it to Pastor Floyd and his team on October 1, 2000. We continued, again without fanfare, to do the ministry of reconciliation. Several of the indicated actions from my assessment were successfully implemented. A simple example was the first-time recognition of Dr. Martin Luther King's birthday in January of 2001. There were numerous other ideas put in play to help encourage and facilitate cross-cultural worship within the normal flow of ministry at Springdale.

On April 13, 2000 we launched the first cross-cultural Bible study (BASIC) in our home in Springdale, Arkansas. As noted, this was a blessed experience. The models developed in Ohio were now successfully in use in Arkansas. We learned quickly that most of the insights were immediately transferable. A week before the in-home group was launched, Dan Lehman, minister of home fellowship groups, wrote an article in the VISION a weekly publication of First Baptist Springdale. Dan said after describing the key logistic details, "The name of the group clues you into the mission of this brand new home fellowship: B.A.S.I.C. = Brothers And Sisters In Christ! People from differing backgrounds and life experiences coming together, centered on the word of God, for the purpose of growing in Christ and encouraging each other in the journey. . . I believe that God is going to do great things under the leadership of the Witherspoons, and that lives will be changed through this ministry."[49]

Later that same year, we started the BASIC Sunday school class on the church campus. As previously discussed, this class was also extremely successful and grew to be one of the largest classes across the entire ministry. Pastor Floyd and I reviewed progress and shared perspectives often.

One of the things we both appreciated most was how the small group efforts were translating into membership within the church. Soon another BASIC small group was formed on the University of Arkansas campus. A young man who I mentored, and who was a member of our in-home small group—Darren—was the prime mover in starting the U of A group. Darren was a dynamic young man completely sold out to the gospel of Jesus Christ. Darren, an African American, teamed up with another dynamic young man named Will who is Caucasian. Together, they kicked off the group and modeled the principle of shared leadership. This small group grew rapidly.

After just a few months of meeting together, the U of A group had blossomed to about forty participants. When I was invited to speak at one of their bible study sessions I was blown away by what I saw! I arrived a bit early and chatted with the group leaders. This group also enjoyed the support of a couple of organizers from Campus Crusade for Christ. So we all met together and discussed how the class was progressing.

Soon the participants began to arrive. What blew me away was the incredible diversity of the participants and the fact more and more kept coming. Having been so impressed by Darren and Will I was not ready for how strong some of the young co-eds were in their leadership ability and love for the Lord. This small group also had some amazing young women on fire for the faith and bold in their presentation of that faith. That night, we fellowshipped for hours and my soul was filled with joy as these young folks shared deeply about their faith and sang to the Lord with soul and energy. We had church that night.

I'm told by friends who work actively in collegiate ministry that groups tend to be very small in size and they often tend to lack the depth of intimacy we saw with this group of young people. This class flourished and became, for me, another example of the power of cross-cultural worship and bible study. The level of penetration and engagement was very similar to what I had experienced before in multiple small groups. By now, we knew we were onto something special. The Lord was teaching us, repeatedly, there was great power in the idea of cross-cultural worship and bible study. Again we were witness to the no holds barred engagement across racial and ethnic barriers afforded by the model of cross-cultural worship; that is, integration—penetration—reconciliation.

Darren and I communicated frequently about the progress of this BASIC class on the U of A campus. I was continually encouraged by all the Lord did through this young man and his colleagues. I took note of how they had applied the principle of shared leadership and how they had implemented quite successfully the model of integration, penetration and reconciliation. It was also very exciting to see the model worked well without me as teacher.

My learning at Springdale was rich. I thank the Lord for how he grew us deeper in what it meant to worship Him in spirit and in truth. In addition to the work we did in the church at Springdale, there were many opportunities to apply what we were learning in cross-cultural worship. My good friends Marcus Carruthers (at one time on the staff of First Baptist Church of Springdale and now senior pastor at the Dwelling Place), and Ron Harris (one of the most gifted grass roots Christian organizers I have ever met) were also passionate about reconciliation in the church. Both these men are leading active Christian ministries now in the Northwest Arkansas area.

We often met and prayed for God's people to be open to the ministry of reconciliation. Throughout our time in Arkansas the Lord continually provided opportunities for me to share what we were learning. I was often invited to preach or to teach in the area churches and in secular settings as well.

By the time we left Arkansas in June 2003 we had witnessed a visible impact upon the Church at Springdale. We had also extended a strong testimony into the community for the cause of Christ. Karen and I worked through our small group activities and through the behind the scenes efforts with Pastor Floyd and his leadership team. Through strong associations with other preachers like Marcus and Ron, our ministry effort extended deeply into the community and beyond. I felt the Lord had us right in the very center of His will. We were learning and applying cross-cultural worship, bible study and fellowship. God was using us and I could see even bigger efforts on the horizon for our work in Northwest Arkansas.

The International Story

Sometimes the Lord exposes us to a new thing to show us the limitations of an old thing. My experience, along with my family, at the International Baptist Church (IBC) of Singapore was such a thing. Prior to this experience, my understanding of cross-cultural worship grew tremendously and some of the learning is captured in the preceding pages. I have wondered, at times, why I did not write this book earlier. The key principles and many of the most profound observations have been with me for many years.

I now know this book could not have been written earlier because God was still planning to take me so much deeper than I had imagined at any prior point in my life. It is now abundantly clear the experience at "IBC" was an essential element in my understanding and growth regarding the biblical imperative for cross-cultural worship. While it may not be a totally fair comparison, I compare this part of my journey to the deepening impact of the Apostle Paul's experience on the road to Damascus and the Apostle Peter's experience on the rooftop of Simon the Tanner's house.[50]

Don't get me wrong, I do not presume to elevate myself by comparing my experience to these great stalwarts of the faith. My intent is simply to express a personal and profound realization that despite ones current level of enlightenment on any spiritually significant subject, God often has another, deeper level of understanding to offer. This is clearly the case for me.

God knew I needed to move to Singapore and to experience my own dusty road or rooftop experience. God also knew I needed to take this journey to deeper understanding in a place where there are no dusty roads and where no one spends time on rooftops. Singapore is perhaps the cleanest city in the world and one of the most modern or technologically advanced. Dusty roads are just not part of the experience. Rooftops, though sometimes wonderfully decorated or covered in natural greenery, are not places where people go for daytime excursions. Singapore is equatorial and the daylight sun, if experienced without the benefit of shade, can be devastatingly hot! So clearly the venue would likely be different in my case compared to the way God revealed his message to Peter and Paul.

So how do the experiences of Paul and Peter relate to my going to Singapore? I'm so glad you asked. There are three key experiential parallels. We three were traveling for a different purpose than where God wanted to take us; neither of us had really ever imagined the possibilities God had already seen for our administration of the gospel; each of us left the experience with a broadened mindset toward the mandate for cross-cultural worship and fellowship. Let us consider each of these three points as I share with you the IBC experience in Singapore.

When I was growing up, one of the realities of our community was most preachers were bi-vocational. They maintained secular jobs in addition to their church ministries. The practical drivers for this were churches often could not afford to pay enough for pastors to meet all their financial obligations and churches needed leadership skills often resident in those who were employed by the public and private sectors. It was often practical for these preachers to work at both "jobs" providing a win-win-win for the preacher, the secular employer and the church.

Today, this practice is still done but it is often viewed with less receptivity by congregants and secular employers. Some secular employers bristle at the prospect of employees also serving in church leadership because it could detract from their service to the company. As companies become evermore competitive they push for increasing employee productivity. Data shows people work longer hours and sleep fewer hours than any prior point in the modern era. If employers can rid their employees of outside interests then it stands to reason more of the employee's time could be given to building the company's business. Fortunately, some employers are also realizing employees with robust interests outside work tend to be happier, and ultimately more productive at work than those who have no life outside work.

Perhaps more relevant is the response within some Christian circles toward bi-vocational ministers. Today there is much more of a ministry bias toward what is being called "full-time Christian service." This, I believe is being driven by a few key factors. First, there are more very large churches—sometimes called mega-churches. These churches are setting the agendas for how "church is done" as congregations look for the working models to emulate. Of course, the working models are judged primarily on the basis of size following the premise that God must be blessing these ministries and condoning their practices as evidenced by their growth. The mega-churches, supported by much larger annual budgets, tend to compensate their staff ministers at levels which cover more, and sometimes all of their financial obligations.

Another reason full-time service is so emphasized is many preachers seek to distinguish themselves from others in the ministry. I hear the full-time distinctive being used as a status indicator. If you are not serving in a "full-time" pastorate, it is often implied you are either not serious about the ministry or just choosing to operate at a "lower level" of commitment. I have never subscribed to this line of thinking. I guess it is because I grew up among some of the most committed pastors I have ever met. It was tough on these servant leaders as they labored to meet the demands upon their time and energy, but I never got the impression they struggled as if serving two masters.

I too have chosen the bi-vocational route. I work in a very challenging and demanding environment at Procter & Gamble and operate a ministry of cross-cultural worship and fellowship. I am sometimes asked, "How do you do it"? This question often comes when people realize how varied my interests appear and how deep my commitment is to whatever aspect of my life they observe. My response is I endeavor to live one life. I do not try and maintain one life at P&G, another life at church, and a different life in other settings. My motivations, the things that drive me, tend to be the same regardless of where I am and what is currently occupying my attention and effort.

While I am not trying to make a detailed proof or justification of bi-vocational leadership, I am suggesting it is a viable option for yesterday and today. Key biblical leaders often retained their professional occupations as fishermen, tent-makers, accountants, doctors, etc. and strong leaders today are doing the same. My attitude is all Christians are compelled to be "full-time" in their service of the Lord. When we try and operate in secular settings as though we have suspended our Christianity we get into huge and often irreconcilable conflicts. I raise this point about bi-vocational service because it helps to illustrate how God sometimes takes us places we never imagined, for reasons we never understood, to accomplish things we never knew we could do. Such is the case with my journey to Singapore.

We moved to Singapore in June 2003 when I was appointed to lead P&G's customer-facing operations in southern Asia. Asia is a very dynamic and exciting place to live and work. Prior assignments and experiences had given me deeper exposure to the western hemisphere, but Asia was a whole new opportunity for me to grow in our business of fast-moving consumer goods.[51] I knew there was also an opportunity for me to learn more about the eastern cultures and apply this learning to my ministry in the church. Before we moved to Singapore, my wife and I took a pre-decision trip in April of 2003. We focused on finding a church and a school for our children—following the pattern we established many years before. We found the right school and the right church during that trip.

Prior to the pre-decision trip, the Lord was already paving the way for us to serve at IBC. A few weeks before we flew over to Singapore our church in Arkansas—First Baptist Springdale—hosted a missionary commissioning service for the Southern Baptist Convention. Seated next to us, during the conference, were Dr. Rankin and his wife Bobbie. Dr. Rankin was head of the convention's mission work in Asia and had spent considerable time in guess where—Singapore. The Rankins shared with us how we must visit IBC and work with the senior pastor, Dr. David Packer who, along with his wife Lana, was leading a unique and dynamic ministry there.

Somehow I had it in my mind the key purpose for moving to Asia was to serve customers and consumers for P&G, but God had in mind another, equally important reason for my going there. Just like Paul (then called Saul) thought he was going to Damascus to round up and arrest Christians and later learned he was there to meet the Lord, I had seen only a part of God's plan for my journey. I was not only going to Singapore to live and work, but to worship—and that on a whole new level.

International Baptist Church of Singapore is unique. Perhaps the very first thing one will notice on Sunday morning is the extraordinary ethnic diversity of the congregation. There are over forty five nations represented among the membership. This is a far cry from what I had experienced in my prior churches in the U. S. and Germany. God showed me a new set of optics. Instead of longing for integration—the first phase of the cross cultural worship model—it was already wonderfully provided. The eleven o'clock worship hour was not the most segregated hour in Singapore as it had been in America. Instead, it was a beautifully colorful panorama of people dedicated to serving and worshipping our Lord and Savior—Jesus Christ. From that very first visit until this current moment I have been enthralled with the study of this unique Christian setting.

This experience helped me to realize God already had a model for integration. The quality of such integration was beyond what I had previously imagined. I liken the experience to Peter's rooftop vision because he knew God's Word was relevant beyond the Jew. After all, he had seen Christ's engagement of non-Jews as previously discussed in the case of the Samaritan woman. Perhaps Peter thought the Jewish people and a few of those from among the Gentiles would receive the Holy Spirit. However, it is probable he was still limited by the paradigm of a mostly Jewish body of believers in Christ. If he held this view, as is clearly implied by his recorded activities leading up to

Acts chapter 8, it was challenged by his experience among the Samaritans in chapter 8 and shattered by the rooftop experience in chapter 10.

The Lord gave Peter a vision of a great sheet being lowered from heaven. The sheet was gathered together at the four corners and containing something inside. Peter, being hungry at the time he began to see this vision was confronted with all manner of beasts of the field and fowl of the air to take for food. Peter initially rejected the food on the basis that it was unclean—that is, not prepared according to the ritual of Jewish tradition. It turns out the vision was a lot less about food and more about the human condition. Peter later realized God was showing him a deeper truth. Peter was thinking about the issue of eating food he considered unclean and God was showing him the possibilities of worship with people he had previously considered unfit. He later preached a sermon extolling the virtue of cross-cultural worship!

I too understood the concept of integration as a critical first step to cross-cultural worship and fellowship. However, I was limited by a framework of "black and white" Christians coming together across racial barriers. This was admirable, but it was not the full picture of how God wanted to use me in ministry. The American civil rights movement was a movement of integration. With Dr. Martin Luther King and a host of other clergymen as key leaders, this movement had a decisively spiritual core element. Much of the movement was conducted via the Church. One of the methods broadly employed was the use of songs to communicate the double meaning of spiritual truth and social strategy.

One of the key songs used for this purpose was, "We Shall Overcome." The Bible refers to the Christian as an "over comer" so the song drew from this great truth and emphasized the expected outcome of their non-violent struggle for social justice in America. The song says, "We shall overcome, we shall overcome, we shall overcome some day . . . deep in my heart, I do believe, we shall overcome some day." If this powerful refrain describes the "what" of the civil rights movement, the verse describes the "how." The song continues,

"Black and white together, black and white together, black and white together some day . . . deep in my heart I do believe we shall overcome some day."

This song was sung often, especially in churches, and is still in broad use today. Black and white together is a wonderful picture, but God brought me to Singapore to show me it is only a fraction of what he means by cross-cultural worship.

So what happened in Singapore? How did God take me deeper in my understanding of cross-cultural worship and fellowship? What does this have to do with you, your church and your ministry for the Lord Jesus Christ? These are good questions to consider in this next section where we go much deeper into the IBC story.

Going Deeper at IBC

Having followed our established pattern, Karen and I located a school for our children and a church home for our family before consummating the move to Singapore. Though we had moved or relocated ten times prior as a family, this was our first international move together. As you might expect it was an eye-opening experience from the outset. Since we had never lived in either of our home towns since we wed, there was always a bit of distance between us and our extended families. We had become accustomed to living away from family, but getting together on holidays and other special occasions. We were always close enough to reach family quickly in an emergency, but far enough that no one dropped in unannounced.

The challenge of getting together with family would now go to a new extreme. Singapore is about as far from Indiana and Tennessee where our extended families are located as you can get and still be on the earth. I often describe the distance to Singapore as going so far . . . that if you went any further you would start coming back!

In some ways, the distance from the US to Singapore is indicated in the social contrasts between the two places. America strongly emphasizes the rights of the individual while Singapore elevates the rights of the society. This insight bears significantly upon the quality of interaction between Americans and Singaporeans. Singapore is famous for its many rules and regulations. America, while it also has many rules, is famous for its freedom. America like many western cultures values individualism; Singapore like many eastern cultures values conformity. Here is my admittedly over-simplified observation of how this dynamic plays out in relationships between Americans and Singaporeans: the former is more adaptive or principle-based and the latter is more strict or rule-based. Of course, this is a generalization and, therefore, left alone as a truth in itself, it would become a prejudice. My intent is not to espouse prejudice or bias, but to acknowledge the power of this and other such insights in bringing cross-cultural worship and fellowship to life.

There are many other differences, some equally profound, which bear upon the quality of relationship attainable between Americans and Singaporeans. I will not examine further those differences, but these and other insights have shaped my understanding of how to do the work and ministry of reconciliation in this context. There are also many similarities between the two nations. Perhaps one of the most notable is the significant racial and ethnic diversity among the populations. America has been called the "melting pot" which is fairly descriptive of the variety of people groups in that nation. As discussed earlier, the checkered history of race relations in America has not made it any authority on how to manage cultural integration.

If America is a melting pot or a soup of sorts, then Singapore is a tossed salad of racial diversity. Parts of inner-city America are completely intertwined with people of variant backgrounds. Other parts stand in stark contrast with well-preserved segregation of races and even ethnic groups. Though such segregation is getting increasingly difficult to maintain some are still trying. Singapore, on the other hand, actively facilitates a balance of racial and ethnic representation in all sectors of society. Through immigration and social policy efforts the whole island is like a giant tossed salad. You have a delicious variety of people groups present, but they are visually distinctive. Most neighborhoods are rich in racial and ethnic diversity as are most places of business, industry and service. I believe this bodes well for the church because it enhances the probability of realizing the first phase of the cross-cultural worship model—integration.

When we moved to Singapore, given our huge interest in cross-cultural worship and fellowship, it was like putting a kid in a candy store. As a student of cross-cultural worship it has been an unbelievable practicum for me.

Though Singaporean society is so wonderfully integrated, it is surprising how segregated some of the churches can be. Most often, the segregation is based upon the language spoken in the worship services. Since many people speak Mandarin, Cantonese, Hindi, Bahasa, Korean, Japanese or other languages they often prefer to worship and teach the Bible in their mother tongue. However, almost everyone in Singapore speaks English and most of the Christian churches do use English as the primary language.

At International Baptist we have three Sunday worship services conducted in English and all the church administration is in English. We also have weekly worship services in Tagalog for Filipinos, Bahasa for Indonesians and our women's ministry reaches many additional language groups through English as a second language (ESL) classes each week. Around the halls of IBC you can hear many languages spoken. You might expect nothing less from a church with over forty five nations represented in its membership.

So let me return to the question of how God took me deeper in my understanding of cross-cultural worship through the experience at IBC. When we arrived, like most people new to an area, we wanted to observe the church in operation. We found the worship services, the Sunday school and the programs of the church quite to our liking. The daily operation of IBC was decidedly American, but with an Asian look and feel. Quickly, we began to establish relationships and make new friends in the church. Karen and I developed a strong relationship with David and Lana Packer who led the ministry at IBC. We also connected quite well with other American families like Tom and Cheryl Linton who were our next door neighbors and long-time members of IBC.

However, since it was easier to make friends with fellow Americans, we focused on meeting more of the people from other places. Our fellowship extended to other strong Christians like Dev and

Sheena from India, Edwin and Jennifer from Singapore, Filipinos, Brits, Australians and many more people from around the world. This was the first time I enjoyed such ready access to Christians from so many backgrounds. What a privilege those early days at IBC was for my family and for me. Almost instantly I appreciated the lesson God was teaching me in the power of "integration." Of course, I had seen the power of integration in the US, but this was a whole new level. It opened my eyes to a new set of possibilities. I thought, for the first time in my ministry life, I could get the cross-cultural worship model going without having to invest so heavily in integration. Do you remember our definition for integration? Integration is the conscious effort to bring different races into physical proximity for corporate worship and fellowship.

At IBC, the people were already in close proximity and they were already in such proximity for the purpose of corporate worship and fellowship. God was teaching me a new breadth of integration. God was expanding me by exposure to a little slice of heaven. I can now better appreciate John the Revelator's vision of "a great multitude that no one could count, from every nation, tribe, people and language" more than ever before.[52] IBC may be among a small and unique group of churches in the world with its level of internal diversity and the reinforcing nature of its external environment. God also taught me integration is not enough.

Just a Little Deeper at IBC

It is funny how God works. He opens and closes doors to the believer as a way of directing the path of our faith experience. Dr. Packer, from the time we joined IBC, had been talking to me about getting involved in leadership quickly. However, it never seemed to happen as pressing matters would take up both our attention. When we would meet for a meal or speak on the phone we always discussed the ministry and the enormous opportunity for IBC to be a beacon of hope to all who passed through this great port city. Dr. Packer, who had also served many years as a missionary to Philippines, had a heart for Asia and service abroad. He had led IBC through a major expansion program including completion of a fine, new worship facility in a strategic location near the city center. I had often shared with David my thoughts on cross-cultural worship and fellowship. We agreed this was a clear and present opportunity at IBC.

In less than a year after we joined IBC, the Packers were called to serve at another church outside Singapore. We never got to work together in implementation of the ideas we discussed. From the moment the Packers left, the pace of our involvement at IBC rapidly accelerated. We seemed to be at the right place at precisely the time God wanted to use us. As I reflect upon it there are scores and scores of exposures and interventions God used to truly engage me in cross-cultural worship and fellowship at IBC. Most of my experiences were under the fire of direct conflict in the church. I was constantly in a mode of observing, interpreting and intervening to help lead IBC from integration to penetration. Do you remember our definition of penetration? Penetration is the process of gaining subsurface insight into the core values and felt needs of people from another racial heritage. For all its integration, I discovered IBC was sorely lacking and desperately in need of penetration. And this is why God had us in this place at this particular time.

Shortly after joining the church we attended a church business meeting. We expected to be in and out within one hour and off to dinner in the downtown area. As the meeting unfolded, it was evident there was a major rift in the church. To our amazement, key leaders in the church board were disagreeing over material being presented to the members. Since the leadership was at odds on several points there was little hope all members would be on one accord. The meeting degenerated into a long string of debates and arguments with no apparent end in sight. The situation seemed one big hopeless mess. I said very little and tried earnestly to listen for understanding to all the points of view espoused on all the topics being discussed.

As best I could discern, there were multiple levels of disagreement. First, and perhaps most important, there was discord among the leadership board. From the meeting we could all see that several decisions of the board had less than unanimous consent. In fact, as more of the board members spoke out, we could see the board was nearly split down the middle.

A second issue was the appearance of groups within the membership supporting both of the "sides" within the board. As the meeting progressed, these groups or factions crystallized their arguments at opposing ends of the spectrum. By the positioning, tone and word choices used, I felt both groups painted themselves into distinctive and unchangeable positions. What was curious about these groups was they were both somewhat organized with a "grass roots" look and feel. What a sad commentary we observed when seeing such factionalizing and fracturing efforts within the body of Christ.

The third level of disagreement was seen in a larger group of members who were neither in the formal or grass roots leadership. They were either oblivious to the issues or they were shocked by the behavior being displayed or both. Many of these members would later share with me a consistent theme of disappointment, disdain and even disgust at behavior they felt was clearly inappropriate for a church business meeting. I was in the third group like so many others. However, I was more disappointed than disgusted. As I listened to the various arguments I found the whole situation quite instructive.

In a strange way, this wonderfully and uniquely integrated church I described earlier was like other churches I had heard about or personally known. This church was not without its own character flaws. The period of strife in this body of believers followed a familiar pattern. Individuals developed issues with each other and left them unresolved; these issues festered and like parasites attached themselves to other larger issues; people who had individual issues chose not to work through their problems according to the grievance process outlined in the Bible; instead, very strong opinions laced with bias were presented in open forum supported by others who either co-signed the issue being raised or allowed the issue to serve as surrogate for other issues they had with the same person or group. What do you get when this pattern unfolds in any church setting? You get a holy mess!

Before we proceed, it may be instructive to review the proper pattern for conflict resolution in the church. One of the key passages is found in Matthew 18. In this passage, Jesus is teaching on appropriate behavior when we face some of life's stressful situations. Beginning in verse 15 Jesus says, "If your brother sins against you, go and show him his fault, just between the two of you. If he listens to you, you have won your brother over. But if he will not listen, take one or two others along, so that every matter may be established by the testimony of two or three witnesses. If he refuses to listen to them, tell it to the church; and if he refuses to listen even to the church, treat him as you would a pagan or a tax collector."[53]

The problem with that business meeting is it was out of order. Jesus said the pattern for conflict resolution was an escalating process with multiple stages. First the person who feels he was wronged goes to the offender to work it out; second one or two arbitrators or witnesses are brought in to help; third it is taken to the whole church. The problem was we were seeing a stage three resolution attempt when stages one and two had not been properly executed.

My intent, in this section, is not to recount all those meetings, discussions and electronic interactions. Instead, I want to pick up a few of the most salient points for our consideration. I also want to share what we learned in applying the biblical principles of Matthew 18 and the simple model of cross-cultural worship to the challenges IBC faced in this period of discord.

So here I am, sitting in a church business meeting with my wife, observing the pain and embarrassment which so often accompanies our failure to follow the patterns for Christian living outlined so clearly in the Bible. This meeting was one in a series of meetings and discussions all designed to make points of great importance to small groups within the church while missing the points so crucial to the entire church. Groups of people were advocating everything from terminating staffers to splitting the church! Eventually, an experienced pastor was engaged to arbitrate among the leadership. This process was not successfully completed. Eventually, some members would stand before the church and apologize for their part in the situation. However, some of the most damaging statements and claims were not immediately put to rest.

The church continued with business meetings as leadership tried to unify the people on a common way forward. These meetings were often extremely contentious. In one particular business meeting, when things had badly degenerated, I decided to speak. Prior to this point, I had been more of an observer. Still a relatively new member, and certainly no expert on the inner workings of this church, I thought silence was the appropriate posture to take at the time. However, as a result of my prior quiet observation, I was not viewed as advocating for any position or any side in the discussions. In this meeting, there was a controversy on whether the meeting itself should even be conducted. Since neither of the leaders who would normally chair the meeting was present, the assembly was in need of someone to chair the meeting. I had not said much, but I had suggested there was a way to reconcile some of the key differences being espoused by various groups in the church. As the meeting drew near its close, or more accurately as it almost died of natural causes, someone suggested I chair the meeting. I agreed to chair the meeting—with certain stipulations. I insisted upon a respectful hearing of opinions by all present; established use of the rules of order including the formal authority of the chair; and appointed a "sergeant at arms" to help escort anyone who became unruly to another room outside the meeting location. All my stipulations were agreed by the members present so we did proceed. The meeting ended with a much calmer tone and we were dismissed in prayer.

All this seemed to work. From that point forward, we continued with meetings to discuss the issues and never again had any exhibits of disrespectful behavior in business meetings. It pains me to write of the extreme discord within the church, but the lessons are too rich and far too relevant to omit. My desire is by painting a realistic and historically accurate picture of what happened the learning can be more readily absorbed. By now, from your own experience, you may already be aware that church congregations are imperfect. Someone has aptly stated, "There are no perfect churches." I think this is true because they are populated with imperfect people.

So let us now look at a few of the specific challenges we faced and the actions we took to find and employ the best possible remedies. With my background and ministry focus, it soon became clear to me I should get very actively involved in bringing resolution to the issues we faced at IBC. I took a series of actions designed to establish the facts, articulate the issues, establish a way forward, enroll all parties in productive debate and discussion, drive resolution to open issues, and restore harmony in the church. My approach was to be simple: I would try and restore proper order to the short-term conflict using the principles embedded in Matthew chapter 18. Additionally, I would use the cross-cultural worship model to address the longer-term and underlying causes of the disunity and discord.

Deeper Still at IBC

I thought the first thing to do was to try and understand the issues and to get much more in tune with the arguments and logic beyond the recommendations various groups and key individuals were making to the congregation. As mentioned, some of these recommendations were drastic to the point of calling for terminations of staff ministers and even splitting of the church. Though there were many recommendations, I thought by addressing the most severe (terminating and dividing) we could get to the root causes of all the major issues. In my work with the most vocal leaders, I found some things you might expect. For example, it was clear there were sides to the issues and each side had its own version of historical events. I had learned long before that no matter how thin you slice the bologna it still has another side. I withheld judgment about the merit of either argument, but focused my effort on getting those involved to clearly articulate their points of view. This was not an easy task, nor was it a quick one. I knew, however, this would be required to move us forward to the desired outcome of the restoration of unity and harmony. So I went deeply into each side's version of events and focused on why they thought the issues were so significant the only remedy was to divide the church.

One thing I certainly did not expect was the sides were defined more along racial or national lines. The whole issue had been grossly over-simplified to a disagreement between the Singaporeans and the expatriates—more specifically, it was a clash between the "locals" and the "expats." This is how people were describing it. This is how ideas were being presented. I would hear people say, "The locals want it this way" or "The expats think that way." Strangely, this wonderfully diverse congregation was being wedged apart by prejudice and bias. This happened for several reasons. First, there was actual prejudice in the hearts of some members toward other members. Second, some found it easier to ascribe opposing views to whole groups of people than to actually understand individual opposing views. Third, there was a complete breakdown in productive discussion between those with opposing views. All the ingredients for the worst type of explosive division of a church were present. It felt like I had drifted back in time to experiences in America when racial tensions were strained beyond safe limits.

One of the early meetings I had was with a group of Singaporean members who were being called "The locals" by others in the church. I spent hours with a few key members from this group over many meetings. I met face to face, one on one, in large groups, with small groups, and read literally hundreds of pages of documents which formed the basis for their positions about the state of things at IBC. I had similar interactions with others in the church being called "expats."[54]

Through all these exchanges I ended up being the one person who knew most about the issues from all the relevant sides of the bologna. It was an unenviable position. The personal emotional price was significant for me. The deeper I got into the issues, the more I understood how wounded and hurt some of the members felt. The intellectual price was also significant to the point of draining and sapping my energy at times. Perhaps, though, the greatest challenge was the spiritual price I paid as a witness to how division in the church robbed so many of the joy and peace of right relationship with their brothers and sisters. Eventually, some would even begin to lose their joy in worshipping God and spreading the gospel.

So what did we learn? The most important learning was the power of penetration as a key step in cross-cultural worship and fellowship. The great irony of this situation was the church failed to leverage its exceptional strength of integration, and this neglected strength nearly became a weakness. The pursuit of individual interests gave rise to separatism, and this led to an almost inevitable prejudice driven by increasing lack of interaction. Let me share six insights we used to move the congregation and its leaders from the path of destruction described above to a new and better place. The first three points are my key learning from the steps or missteps of leaders and the second three points were taken from learning among the membership.

Three Learning Points for Leaders

As mentioned, I spent a considerable time in observation of the arguments raised and the personal convictions of those who presented these arguments. I read hundreds of pages of written correspondence and spoke to a large cross section of leaders from the church staff, deacons, committee heads and the "grass roots" leaders among the congregation who felt empowered to represent the members on various issues. Sadly, somehow the authority and esteem for the office of senior pastor had been denigrated in this period of strife.

The church had become factionalized on several levels. On one hand there was division among groups of members. This was being grossly over-simplified as a contest between the expats and the locals. I can imagine this sounds silly to you, but I assure you it was serious stuff. Folk even had to declare which "camp" they were in. On the other hand there was division among the leaders. This was rooted in serious disagreement over a number of issues facing the church. Eventually, the leadership and congregational divisions began to merge. This was the classical recipe for a church split.

Here are my three key observations about the leadership behavior and the associated learning I now take from the experience. First, I saw the power of transparency as a bridge between opposing viewpoints. One of the most effective fuels for division in the church was perceived and real secrecy. In a Baptist church, the congregation has greater authority to determine its direction as a local body than the churches of many other denominations. This is often called "congregational rule" and is a key tenet of Baptist polity. Generally, when there is harmony in the church congregational rule is not mentioned. However, when things go awry or when the church faces difficult challenges or decisions this principle of authority is often raised. This is not unique to IBC, but it came into sharp focus at IBC.

In 2004 confusion and frustration peaked at IBC. As we came to the end of 2004 a new leadership team was installed consisting of a completely new Deacon Board which I chaired and a new Interim Senior Pastor—Dr. Luis Pantoja, Jr. There were numerous areas of confusion related to the notion of congregational rule which the new leadership had to address quickly and effectively. As we began to work on the issues we took on the twin tasks of finding a permanent senior pastor through a special search committee which I led and revising the outdated constitution through another special committee led by Andrew Hanam, a member of the newly installed Deacon Council. One of the big challenges for the constitution committee was to bring crystal clarity to the "delegation of authority" in decision making. It is true in a Baptist church the congregation holds the final authority in decisions facing the church. When churches are small it is a common practice to convene the entire congregation for most if not all key decisions to be taken. It is also true once a congregation reaches a certain size it is no longer practical to convene the church to consider and vote on every decision taken. Larger churches will make hundreds of decisions each week. If all these had to come before a congregational meeting for vote the activity of the church would be greatly retarded or hindered.

To address this challenge, churches would need to clarify the rules governing the delegation of authority. This clarity is formally expressed in the church constitution. As mentioned we undertook a major effort to rewrite the constitution of International Baptist Church of Singapore. Our previous constitution was a fairly weak document, sufficiently vague on many key points to permit argument for or against nearly any action the church might take. To a large degree, we needed to start over with a new document bearing tighter language and closer adherence to the New Testament. Andrew Hanam and his committee did a fantastic job leading timely completion of this work. The entire revision process was completed in 2005 and the key changes were activated as we began the 2006 budget year. By this committee's effort, decision rights and escalation of grievances have been greatly clarified. As part of this new clarity, we restored the authority and dignity of the office of the senior pastor.

Perhaps one of my biggest learning points from this entire experience was the power of transparency. One of the reasons factions gathered so much steam at IBC was the previous poor flow of information and sometimes slow or inconsistent messaging from leadership on matters of importance to members. This helped to undermine leadership credibility and reduce the effectiveness of leadership's intended actions. As a new leadership team our answer to this challenge was full transparency. Once the new leadership team took office, we began to proactively share key decisions of the board in writing with all members. The board met every two weeks and published key decisions in the Sunday worship service bulletin. This had a dramatic and almost immediate effect of reducing the noise and confusion about what leadership was doing and where the church was heading.

Without transparency it was easy for people to imply secrecy or even deception was at work. The old board was constantly bombarded with certain "findings" which were believed intentionally kept from the members. Sadly, these discoveries would be shared in open session of church-wide business meetings with dramatic and damaging effect. Once these findings were exposed the board would be distracted with a need to suddenly address a new issue. Every moment spent addressing the new issue was time away from solving the pressing needs already under consideration. Lack of transparency was a true Achilles heel for the previous board. As a new board we turned transparency from a weakness to strength.

In addition to regularly publishing key board decisions and activities, we also held numerous open discussions among the members. These open discussions were widely attended at first, especially by the more vocal members. As time passed, these meetings saw reduced attendance and eventually they were no longer needed. Members moved from having an undercurrent of skepticism to a normalized level of trust in leadership's judgment driven by disclosure of relevant information.

The second leadership learning was the unintended consequences of loyalty. Loyalty can be a good thing because it can help facilitate a unified train of thought, and unity of thought can translate to unity of purpose which may ultimately lead to unified action. As we have earlier discussed, unity in the Church is of extreme importance. You might say it is a mission critical attribute. Now loyalty is very often viewed as equivalent to support. If someone is loyal to me as a leader, following this line of thinking, then they are supportive of my ideas and plans. Again, this is a good thing because leaders must have the support of followers to be successful in carrying out an agenda. If the leader espouses an idea and others agree with and support the idea, then the idea can more readily be implemented.

The problem with loyalty is it is sometimes misunderstood. Some leaders exert pressure for others to follow and support their ideas out of a sense of loyalty alone. They equate agreement to an idea with support for the leader. This is the point of departure which can make loyalty dangerous. Often, when ideas are supported or rejected it has nothing to do with loyalty. People simply support an idea they believe to be good and appropriate for the situation at hand or they reject an idea which to them lacks merit. When a leader, especially in a church setting, ties too closely another person's support of an idea to their support of the leader himself it causes several problems including the creation of false or unnecessary dilemmas.

The false dilemma is created when a person is made to feel they cannot reject a faulty idea without also rejecting the leader who generated that idea. When this happens it lessens the effectiveness of the leader and the follower. The leader loses effectiveness because they tend to alienate those who disagree. This leaves only those who agree in the presence of the leader. When a leader is surrounded only with people who agree with his views on every matter then he limits the potential of finding and implementing the very best ideas. The follower loses effectiveness too because they either degenerate into being a "yes man" who offers no independent thought or insight or they are removed from the discussion altogether. Adults quickly figure out when they are being pressured to agree with a leader. When they realize their legitimate disagreement with certain ideas is not heard or heeded, they either become angry or they stop offering their ideas.

In the case of IBC, we saw the weakening of leadership effectiveness and the erosion of strong input from those who would be followers. A sort of false dilemma came about on multiple levels. The established leadership of the church was estranged from certain voices within the church. Factions arose along polarizing "ideas" or points of view. Agreement with the leader(s) was evoked as a barometer of loyalty. The so-called grass roots leaders laid claim to ideas and pressured their so-called constituents to agree out of loyalty. It all seems strange now, but we witnessed a parsing of the body of Christ driven in large part by a runaway sense of loyalty! People were pressed to pick a side and once committed, they needed to tow the party line. Groups were organizing around certain ideas in private meetings outside the church. The products of these meetings were proposals for how IBC should move forward and remedy the problems she faced. The proposals were presented in open business meetings of the congregation. Often, these proposals would be met with heated disagreement because they were sprung onto members without the benefit of rigorous debate by people who held opposing views or possessed important missing information.

Politics had entered the church and Christians were faced with a compromising false dilemma: do I express my loyalty to the leader as a "good expat" or a "good local" or do I express the truth without reservation as a "good Christian"? This was the situation many found themselves in at IBC. I call it a false dilemma because a Christian is always obliged to tell the truth. Remember that little line in Exodus which so emphatically states, "Thou shall not lie"?

The strength of personal conviction should be freely expressed in the church. The Bible does not tell us to stop thinking when we become Christians. Our reasoning faculties are not diminished by being saved. So what happened to us? I'll tell you what happened. The pressure of errant loyalty happened. This pressure was real and it caused significant pain and strife among members. Looking back, it is easy to see the folly of this situation. At the time the church was living through this experience I think people genuinely struggled in the false dilemma presented to them.

Based upon my learning in this situation and others, I have developed a watchful eye and an alert ear to leadership cries for loyalty. We must be loyal to Christ and to the truth—which is Christ. Jesus said, "I am the way, the truth and the life." We should be unfaltering in our loyalty to truth because in doing so we honor the Lord Jesus Christ. However, we are not obligated to agree with every idea espoused by another believer regardless of their position or our position in the Church. Any leader who pressures members to accept their point of view based upon loyalty to the leader provides an undesirable form of leadership. Any member of a church who lends their support to an idea which they believe inappropriate or inaccurate does a disservice to themselves and the leader. Ultimately, such a person does a disservice to the cause of Christ.

In my observation, loyalty not only sets up a false dilemma, but it can also act as a lullaby that puts the unsuspecting believer to sleep. Why would I say that? I say it because loyalty gone too far can cause a person to withhold valuable input as though they were asleep during the discussion. Such input would be withheld due to the perceived risk of disagreeing with the leader. An otherwise intelligent person with a legitimate point of view or even a vital piece of new information could be shut out from sharing such perspective. This can lead to the wrong decision and reduce effectiveness of the ministry. In our case at IBC, loyalty to the grass roots leaders perpetuated various ideas predicated upon inaccurate or incomplete data. This is not bad in itself because sometimes decisions must be taken without all the facts being available.

However, I found there were people present in the various factions who had the missing information but did not share it. The reason they withheld those key points of perspective was loyalty. People do not often set out to make poor decisions, nor do they often set out to support poor decisions. However, poor decisions are often propelled by the unintended consequences of loyalty gone too far. New or opposing ideas should be met with assessment for understanding and determination of merit. If a new or opposing idea is appropriate for the situation at hand and is superior to the leader's idea it should be adopted. Under normal circumstances this would happen among fair minded people. But sometimes necessary input is not given. As leaders we must encourage input from among our members. As leaders we must reject the notion that everyone must agree with everything we say or think. As leaders we must learn to diminish or eliminate effects of the loyalty lullaby and keep it from rocking our members to sleep.

So we have talked about transparency. With the exception of confidential counseling or confession information shared privately between clergy and parishioners, church leadership is well advised to engage in full transparency with the members. We have also talked about loyalty. Leaders do an enormous disservice to themselves and their members when loyalty is defined as agreement to everything the leader says or thinks. God places different members in the body with varying experiences and perspectives in order to enable the best course of action for the church. I believe God always enables the superior way forward in any situation, but we do not always see or exercise the plan God has enabled.

The third major learning point for leaders is about the criticality of leadership sensitivity. Through our experience at IBC, I learned to appreciate even more the sensibility of sensitivity. Recently I preached a sermon entitled "Close Enough to Touch." The message was taken from a bible passage in Mark chapter 5. There we find the story of a very sick woman who was healed when she touched the hem of Jesus' garment. In the story, this woman had been sick for twelve years with a condition causing her to hemorrhage incessantly. When she heard Jesus was nearby she made her way to him. A large crowd had drawn around Jesus and the woman was lost in the throng of people. Jesus had earlier been approached by Jairus, a leader in the local synagogue, who asked the Lord's assistance for his dying daughter. Jesus consented to help Jairus and together they began to make their way to the bedside of this twelve year old dying girl.

Along the way to Jairus' house, with the crowd of people still following Jesus, someone reaches out and touches the hem of Jesus' garment. It was later revealed to be the woman who had been bleeding for twelve years. When she touched him, she was immediately made whole and relieved completely of her affliction. The Bible says Jesus realized he had been touched, turned around in the crowd and called out to find the one who had touched him. Eventually, the woman came forward and acknowledged it was she who had touched Jesus. He ministered a few words to her and encouraged her in faith. Then Jesus and Jairus continued on their way.

One of the amazing things about this encounter was that Jesus Christ noticed he had been touched in the first place. Think about it. He is walking in a crowd; he is moving with great intention toward an emergency situation where a little girl is dying; someone comes up behind him and touches his outer garment at the hem. And somehow Jesus notices he had been touched! I am greatly impressed by the way Jesus noticed her touch, acknowledged her faith, and met her needs.

This story captures the enormous sensitivity Jesus Christ had under such stressful conditions to even notice he had been touched. Many of us would not have noticed. Some of us, even had we noticed the touch, would have ignored the opportunity to minister to this woman because of the already pressing matter of Jairus' daughter. Jesus, in this example, modeled the sensibility of sensitivity. Despite being busy with other legitimate attentions; despite being engaged with an important man's personal crisis; he was sensitive to a desperate and depleted woman. In the eyes of many leaders, this woman would be viewed as a distraction. It would be considered by many to show a poor sense of priority management and a profound lack of focus to stop and deal with her problem given the situation. Jesus, however, saw the urgency of her need too. Jesus showed it was not irresponsible to stop and attend her needs. He knew she had physical and spiritual needs warranting his attention. When he stopped to address this woman, Jesus modeled for us as modern-day leaders just how sensible it is to be sensitive to the needs of others.

Through the experience at IBC, I learned afresh the sensibility of such sensitivity. I had been approached earlier by members of the so-called expat group who appealed to me on the basis of affinity. Some among them argued how ridiculous the claims of the so-called locals were. Separately, I had been engaged by some from among the so-called locals who felt I was fair-minded and would actually hear them out.

The more I dug into the issues among our members, the more I understood and was sensitized to the real and perceived needs they each had. Eventually, I came to appreciate the reasons behind the needs and I felt the pain behind the behavior. At IBC, like any other church, people were hurting. They may not have been suffering the level of physical challenge this woman in the bible story faced, but they were hurting all the same. When I engaged those real life situations which members shared with me over many hours of personal discourse, often with tears, I became keenly aware of how important it was to address the concerns.

Leaders must develop, as Jesus had, sensitivity to the hurting of others. Somehow we must sharpen our senses to be able to perceive not only the obvious or the well articulated demands of the vocal mainstreamers, but the nearly imperceptible cries and touches of the needy. Somehow we must be able to reach out, even to pause amid the rush of current priorities and minister to those not in our direct line of sight. Somehow we must become more sensitive.

As I began to invest in listening to the needs of our members, I could see the burden of feeling ignored or marginalized being lifted from their disposition. The more people were heard the more they were encouraged to continue their engagement. Through the often arduous work at IBC we experienced the power of having a heightened sensitivity. Personally, I was changed by this experience. I don't know if I yet have that hem of the garment sensitivity, but I know that is what is required. I don't know if I will always stop when a need presents itself, but I know that is what is desired.

When you consider this learning about transparency, loyalty and sensitivity together, they are a strong collective reminder of the mindset a cross-cultural leader should maintain. You should enable full transparency, avoid the lullaby of loyalty, and adapt the sensibility of sensitivity. When these three are working together in your leadership style you will get the right information from a proper view of loyalty, give the right information in a proper view of transparency, and address more of the right ministry opportunities with a proper view of sensitivity.

Three Learning Points for Members

The learning points for leaders were extremely important for my growth and development in the ministry of cross-cultural worship. I hope you can readily see the collective power of leadership adoption of this learning. The learning for members may be even more compelling. Again I offer three learning points, but instead of describing them as single watchwords like transparency, loyalty and sensitivity, we will use two word movements. My three learning points for members involve the need of each member to sometimes move from surrogates to owners; from positions to principles; and from distinctive to inclusive. Let me explain each of these movements in turn.

First, it is sometimes important to move from using surrogates to being owners. Here is how it works. A surrogate, in this context, is a member of the church who is asked to represent another member's point of view or assumes this responsibility without being asked to do so. An owner is a member who represents their own point of view with others in the church. When IBC was in its most stressful period of division and discord, the Lord decided to use me as a part of the solution. One of the most effective steps I took was to arrange a series of meetings with each of the groups or factions that had emerged in the church. Recall, earlier I said there were so-called grass roots leaders who felt they were empowered to represent the points of view of others. I met with these leaders one on one or in groups of two or three. One of the things I noticed repeatedly was how these leaders would use phrases like, "The people feel" or "Many in the church believe" to give credibility to their arguments. I listened intently to their arguments and parroted back to them what I had heard to confirm my understanding. At times some would even mention to me how they were speaking for another member or how some members had given them a proxy to represent their issue before other members in the church. As you might expect, this made it quite difficult to ascertain whose issue was being addressed and how many people subscribed to this point of view.

Following my discussions with all the grass roots leaders I requested meetings with larger groups within the various factions of the church. In these sessions, I would have the grass roots leaders and those he was representing. To begin each meeting I would clearly establish the ground rules by which the discussion would proceed. One of the ground rules was that each person would have to own their own ideas. In other words they would have to be owners. Everyone present would also have to speak so there would be no free ride on the points made by someone else. They could not introduce an idea as something another person felt or believed. All points being considered would be offered in the first person as "my" idea or something "I" believe to be true. This turned out to be extremely effective. Some of the members present in these discussions clearly moved from surrogate to owner. They learned by experience how important it is to express ones own convictions. They learned that it was not necessary to have a surrogate to carry their perspective to other members.

In one meeting we had leaders and members of two opposing factions present. I allowed leaders to share an overview, but we captured only the individual points shared by members themselves. As those who had previously used surrogates began to express themselves openly, I could see the healing effect. There is something about saying a thing yourself. Tears began to flow. Apologies were given and received. Relationships were being mended.

When members would share their perspectives I would capture their points on large sheets of paper and post them on the walls around the meeting room. In one such meeting we got together opposing groups on a Saturday morning. The discussion went into the early afternoon and we generated sheets of paper all around the meeting room. I had the members from both groups observe the written record of all the perspectives and ask questions to clarify the meaning of each point. Next I had each member to go around the room and mark the points with which they agreed. As you might imagine, this was a huge learning experience for all involved. Some found out they held opinions which were not corroborated by anyone else in their faction or group. Others learned their perspective was also shared by members from the opposing faction. The markings on the posters formed a real time Pareto analysis. We were able to group the issues into buckets and determine who should help resolve them. I followed each of the biggest issues (i.e., those points widely held as true by those present) through to its final resolution and communicated back with those involved.

After a series of these discussions we began to enjoy clear articulation of the issues, ongoing communication about the remedies employed and timely reporting of the resolutions. Following this series of meetings the need for grass roots leadership to represent members' view was greatly diminished. Eventually members started speaking more directly to each other and matters affecting the church were again being brought up in proper forum and with proper decorum. We had gently moved back in line with the grievance process articulated in Matthew chapter 18.

The second learning point for members was about moving from positions to principles. A position is taken when someone espouses a polarizing point of view and makes no allowance for compromise. A principle is taken when a broader view of the issue is permitted and multiple options or possibilities can co-exist. Taking a position is often appropriate in church when it comes to major matters of doctrine. We should not compromise on the matter of whether Jesus Christ is the Son of the Living God or whether this same Jesus Christ arose from the dead on what has come to be celebrated as Easter Sunday. We should not compromise on the inerrancy of scripture or the idea that the scriptures contained in the Holy Bible are the historically accurate and currently relevant revelation of the person of God. On such things we as Christians should take a position. However, we do not need to take an unchangeable position on every point of discussion or decision in the church. Beyond major matters of doctrine, especially on matters where the Bible either does not speak conclusively or is silent altogether, we should be open to grow through the expression of other believers. In such matters we should be guided not by unyielding positions, but by principles. Principles are like guideposts or frameworks for navigating the lesser matters. When one uses dogmatic approaches to lesser matters it can be a real turnoff for most people. We must be careful to acknowledge other possibilities on the lesser matters. We must be willing to adopt principles, grounded in biblical truth much as possible, to govern the handling of the lesser matters of church life.

One of the things which perplexed me about the discord at IBC was how it seemed so formal. The grass roots leaders were extremely organized and they showed up in church business meetings operating with techniques one might expect to see from political parties or labor unions. I often wondered why things were being presented with formal position papers and typed motions. I wondered why lawyers and diplomats in the church were rising to make remarks with a decidedly formal tone.

Then one day it hit me. The formality of all these business meeting presentations was being driven by a somewhat simple reality. Some members were taking up positions when they may have been better served to offer a set of principles. Church documents, including the old church constitution with its inconclusive sections and articles, were being used as proof of the validity of these positions. Why were these positions so vigorously presented and so rigorously defended? They were so presented and defended because if they were accepted, then the group espousing them would be declared right. Of course, as is generally the case with positions, if one group was declared right then the other group must be declared wrong. Positions were introduced so blame could be assigned and offenders could be exposed.

My question in all this was why was it necessary on these lesser matters to declare individuals as right or wrong? We needed to reframe the entire discussion away from assigning blame to finding and implementing solutions. Positions only held us back; they did not help us move forward. With positions the church either had to accept or reject every perspective shared. I could not see the value in forcing people to take a polarizing position on something which was not absolutely conclusive. So we introduced principles to the discussion. We declared those principles up front when the congregation would meet. Sometimes we offered operating principles for how we would conduct thorny discussions. Other times we offered interpretive principles for how we would apply biblical insights, church constitution interpretation or other guidelines with bearing on our discussion topics.

This really seemed to help. It removed the need for members to take positions on matters where multiple remedies could be effectively implemented. Our members began again to hear the voices of others with open minds. Soon people no longer felt they must take sides based upon over-simplified demographic constructs like "expats and locals." They began to listen with empathy and allow discussions to flow toward possibilities and options. Discussions no longer had winners and losers and good ideas had broad based support. Over time we took discussion of lesser matters from positions to principles.

The third learning point for members is moving from distinctive to inclusive thinking and behavior. You may notice I did not say move from exclusive to inclusive although I think it is important to do so. The learning at IBC was not so much about being exclusive. Our vast diversity often made this impractical. It made little sense for a member to present an idea as being true for only a particular group. We did not have the problem of such overt segregation as people disallowing participation at functions or programs of the church. We did not see widespread exclusivity espoused as an approach. However, we did suffer the use of distinctives. A distinctive is used when an idea is presented as indicative of a particular person or group. Sometimes an idea is presented as the way all people of a certain group think. It comes in the form of generalizations like "all the Chinese members want to hear this" or "people who are not from Singapore will never understand that." The danger in this approach is the idea becomes attached to the group or worse; it becomes synonymous with the group. This is the seed of prejudice. By affinity a person is signed onto some idea for which they have no prior knowledge. They may even be associated with an idea with which they wholeheartedly disagree.

So here is a bonus learning point. It is a good reminder for the leaders and the members. The bonus point is balance. Balance is what should come from integration and penetration as we engage in cross-cultural worship. Balance is the new idea. It is the idea which reflects the best of the parts but is made relevant by the whole. Balance is the new music, the new vocabulary, the new programs, the new approaches, the new ways of working which come from the melding of the separate.

The Bible says, "If any man be in Christ he is a new creature, old things are passed away, behold all things are become new." I was thinking about this passage in light of the discussion we just had regarding surrogates, positions and distinctives. If we are supposed to be so new based upon our being in Christ then why are we doing the same old thing we did before we knew the Lord? How can we get so embroiled in discord? Why do we seek a distinctive when an inclusive approach will do just fine? Why do we take a position when a principle will suffice? Why do we sometimes want to send a surrogate when owning our own stuff is more efficient and effective? We do these things because we lack balance. Someone has said, "You can't teach old dogs new tricks." Well we are new creatures who are still trying to apply the old ways.

So the learning for members is also a strong collective reminder of the mindset we should carry into an environment of cross-cultural worship. The adoption of these membership and leadership mindsets or ways of working will have a strong influence upon the effectiveness of the church.

THEN GOD DELIVERED

In the section on our IBC experience I tried to share some of the actual interventions we made and the learning I have taken from the experience. You should not take the impression I am taking credit for all that happened or that I am trying to express some profound personal brilliance or effectiveness which transformed the situation at IBC. The fact is God was the chief architect of what happened at IBC. The Lord used me and others to execute his plan in the life of the church. The specificity provided is designed to help you grasp and appreciate the practical and experiential component of what happened at IBC. I believe, and it has been confirmed by many who were present during this period, the Lord brought about a God-sized transformation at IBC. To God be the glory for all that was accomplished and the new more effective ministry which has emerged in this unique church strategically located in one of the key global gateway cities between the east and west.

The reality of ministry work is God reveals his will to his people through prayer, study of his Word and fellowship with other believers. He raises leaders to carry the oversight responsibility to cast the vision and articulate the execution of his will. He assembles all the right talent, experiences and spiritual gifts among the congregation to carry out successful implementation of his vision. All truly successful churches tap into the vision and utilize the broader base of complimentary talent which God brings together on His timing. This is what happened at IBC.

God Assembled the Right Talent

Let me tell you the rest of the story so you can gain an appreciation for how God brought things together and created a way out of no way. The Lord used people to help transform IBC from a church on the precipice of disastrous split to a church unified in its vision and engaged in cross-cultural penetration. Besides his use of my gifts and talents there were a number of people whom God employed in the transformation of IBC.

I would first mention the 2005 Deacon Council. This group of men was a direct application of the concept of shared leadership. The church elected a slate of twelve deacons to serve for 2005 with a perfect balance among Singaporean members and those from other countries. It was my great privilege to lead this council and serve among these men. Don, Christopher, Andrew, Edwin, Benrio, Cliff, Jeff, Murray, Eastwood, Yanai, Chuck and I had our work cut out for us on so many fronts. The 2005 Deacon Council undertook the huge task of unifying the congregation through intense and prayerful consideration of the open issues coupled with transparent and frequent communication. This council was effective as a unit. We operated very well together by remaining in touch with all segments of the membership. This council brought closure to the interpersonal challenges among the staff, led the much needed revision of the church constitution, and managed the transition of staff leadership as God called new leaders to His service at IBC. I will remember this group of men as one of the most effective groups with whom I have ever worked.

The Lord showed perhaps his greatest provision of leadership for IBC by calling Pastor Luis Pantoja, Jr. to service among us. The 2005 Deacon Council appointed a special search committee to find an interim pastor. I had the opportunity to lead this effort, but it was Dev Sarker, one of the committee members, who made contact with Dr. Pantoja and gained his agreement to serve in this capacity. Dr. Pantoja was on sabbatical from his position as senior pastor of the very large, dynamic ministry at Greenhills Christian Fellowship in Pasig City, Philippines near Manila. God used this strong leader to bring direction to the staff team who were undergoing significant transition. He led, not only from the pulpit where he was an outstanding presenter and defender of the faith, but also in the details of daily life among the members. He visited many of the small groups and it seemed he was present at every event where IBC members were involved. The people of IBC will always be indebted to this great man of God who chose to spend his entire sabbatical in service to another church!

Dr. Pantoja was instrumental in helping the Deacon Council work through the rigorous constitution change effort. One of the changes in the new constitution was the implementation of a new leadership structure which retained the roles of staff leadership and deacons, but added the new role of elder. We formed the first IBC Elder Board with the spiritual oversight of Dr. Pantoja. I was also elected to chair this first group of elders. The board consisted of Andrew, Edwin and I who had previously served on the Deacon Council. We added Tom, Paul and Simon to round out the board along with the new senior pastor. The 2006 Elder Team put the 2005 strategic and tactical choices into effect. IBC emerged in 2006 with a new church constitution, a new Elder team and a new senior pastor.

It was our interim pastor, Dr. Pantoja, who made initial contact with the man who would eventually replace him in the senior pastorate. Dr. Ben Brown, who was serving as senior pastor of BBC Ministries in Klamath Falls, Oregon, was called to serve as the new senior pastor at IBC. Once Pastor Ben was on the ground he began building the new staff leadership team. The Lord brought a new Minister of music and worship, Pastor Alan Moore, and used him mightily to transform the music ministry. Pastor Alan has among other accomplishments been very effective at better integrating the efforts of our Filipino musicians into the broader context of IBC's worship experience. Pastor Ben has made other staff changes and the Lord is clearly blessing the ministry at IBC in visible and invisible ways.

God Gave Us a New Vision

The church is now focused and driving toward a common vision reflecting the unique opportunity at IBC. The vision is modeled on the great commission of Acts 1:8 as IBC seeks to reach Singapore for

Christ as a catalyst to reach all of Asia and be a bridge between East and West. This has been an energizing and unifying vision for the church. God has used this new vision to sharpen the ministry efforts. A big outgrowth of this new vision has been a step function change in our mission work to China and parts of Southeast Asia.

The vision is also helping to get members more active in ministry to the local communities surrounding the church. God has unified his church at International Baptist and IBC is now a vibrant ministry. For those who were present and lived through the change it has left an indelible mark on our lives. The transformation was from an internally focused body losing productivity to a long list of squabbles to a place where the weary traveler can find rest and renewal in the fellowship of the saints.

God has blessed us with a significant increase in the numbers of attendees, new members and baptisms. We have seen growth of participants in virtually all aspects of the ministry at IBC. More important than the numeric growth is the joy one can easily sense in worship among this assembly of brothers and sisters in Christ. There is a new and pleasant feeling which permeates the ministry. I see a more purposeful external focus on winning the lost to Christ. I see a congregation more readily investing in the possibilities which come from establishment of penetrating sub-surface relationships. I see a church clearly more energized by possibilities than constrained by limitations. If you find yourself in Singapore I hope you will stay over the weekend and worship among the people at International Baptist Church. It is truly a little taste of what heavenly worship will be like for the believer.

PRINCIPLES FOR APPLICATION

We have covered much ground and now it is a good time to summarize the key points you should take forward. In your personal approach to the challenge of cross-cultural worship and bible study please apply all that you have found useful on these pages. I pray you have been moved by our argument of biblical and empirical evidence. If not, I hope you at least enjoyed the discussion. I hope you will remember the three steps of the Cross-Cultural Worship Model: integration, penetration and reconciliation. I know it sounds simple, but I can tell you from experience it is easier said than done. To aid in application of this work to your ministry I have also extracted twelve principles from our discussion on cross-cultural worship.

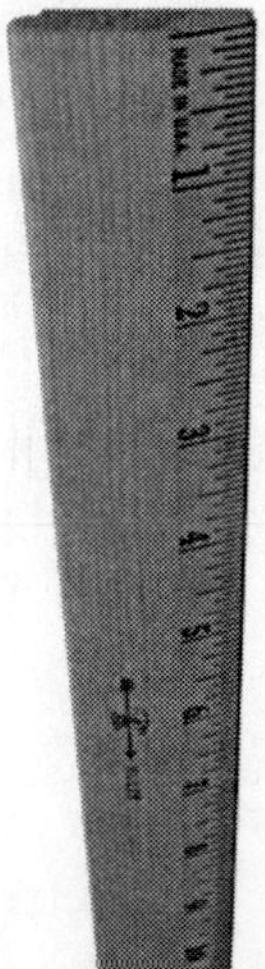

TWELVE PRINCIPLES

1. Intentionality
2. Shared Leadership
3. Touch-ability
4. Personal Observation
5. Divine Reconciliation
6. Proximity
7. Cross Equity
8. Scratch and Sniff
9. Transparency
10. Loyalty Lullaby
11. Sensible Sensitivity
12. Balance

Principle 1: INTENTIONALITY

The principle of intentionality points out our personal and collective responsibility to act on the opportunity for unity. The church must move with "intent" toward cross cultural worship because there is a clear and compelling biblical mandate to do so. Jesus was intentional about cross cultural worship and often went out of his way to involve those who were distanced or disenfranchised. The church should take its clue from the Lord's example and bring proactive effort to the challenge of working across cultures. Intentionality is necessary to overcome the forces which work against unity. If we leave the work of reconciliation to someone else it may never get done in the ministries and communities we serve.

Principle 2: SHARED LEADERSHIP

The principle of shared leadership indicates the power of having a leadership team comprising different cultural backgrounds. With this in place all congregants can see themselves in the future fabric of the ministry. Without it our talk of unity remains theoretical and empty. We may not be able to control who comes to worship with us, but as leaders we can control who works for us and with us in ministry leadership.

The church at Antioch provides a wonderful example of how to do cross cultural worship in the New Testament context. One of the key attributes of the Antioch "startup" was the cross cultural composition of the leadership team. This is an essential insight for modern day reapplication. When leaders surround themselves with only those who look like, think like, and act like themselves they invite limitations upon their ministry. It is important for people to see cross cultural leadership because it indicates inclusion. Our experience also teaches us there is value to "blended beginnings." A blended beginning occurs when you start a new small group or a new committee, council or team with a cross cultural composition. Such groups think more broadly, create more possibilities and often find better solutions than culturally homogeneous groups. They also tend to grow cross-culturally. Shared leadership and blended beginnings are key enablers to an environment of natural and organic cross-cultural growth.

Principle 3: TOUCH-ABILITY

The principle of touch-ability emphasizes just how close we should be to those we serve. Churches active in all areas of a community tend to have a composition representative of the touch points where they invest. If a church is homogeneous, especially in a modern city, it is because they have a ministry which does not "touch" all points in the community. We need to build effective ministries capable of touching all segments of our communities for Christ. Someone has aptly observed how Jesus often ministered with a word, a look or a touch. To minister in this way we must be in touch with those whom we are called to serve. To minister in this way we must be willing to get our hands dirty with the work of ministry. We must even be willing to touch the heretofore untouchable. In short, we must be close enough to touch.

Principle 4: PERSONAL OBSERVATION

The principle of personal observation reminds us to take notice of how we "show up" to other believers. This all begins with you. You must be willing to objectively and critically analyze your own behavior. Learn to see yourself clearly and in context. You may be surprised to find out how you show up among the brethren. Do you put on veneers when you enter the church house? Do you become someone else for the brief time you are in the company of believers? Let me let you in on a secret . . . if you are phony and full of pretense others will see it. They may not say it, but they see it. Learn to see yourself and be yourself especially in the church.

Observe how your church "receives" you on Sunday morning. Ask yourself what your church is doing to make other believers from different races or backgrounds a part of the fabric of the ministry.

Make a list of all the barriers you can identify then ask why these barriers exist and what it would take to remove them? Don't segregate, integrate!

Principle 5: DIVINE RECONCILIATION

The principle of divine reconciliation reminds us that God does the reconciling. He reconciles man to Himself and He reconciles men with each other. It is easy to fall into the trap of somehow thinking we can orchestrate this process entirely through fancy models and techniques. I believe the Lord will honor your honest effort to work cross culturally within the church, but such effort is no guarantee of immediate or sustainable results. The reason to put forward an effort toward reconciliation and cross-cultural worship is straight forward—we do it because it is consistent with the full counsel of New Testament teaching and it is evident in the end game of heavenly worship. We do well to remember our effort, though essential, is borne out of the knowledge that God must actually effectuate the reconciliation. It is God who makes of two the one new man.

Principle 6: PROXIMITY

The principle of proximity suggests our neighbor is not always the one physically closest to us or most like us. Our neighbor can be the closest to us or the furthest away from us. Our neighbor can be just like us or nothing like us. But in any case, our responsibility is to love our neighbor as we love ourselves. It should be easy to love others within the body of Christ, but something constrains us from doing so. I'm not talking about theoretical love. I'm talking about real love, of the kind that bears itself out in real action. Have you ever wondered why we so often stop short of real love when it comes to loving cross-culturally? What is it that keeps us from demonstrating a Christ-like love for one another? Why do we not see and act upon the mandate of cross cultural worship and fellowship? I would suggest it is most often because we lack a proper view of proximity. We lack a correct perspective of who our neighbor is. We are just like all those who passed the man along the Jericho roadside who was beaten and left for dead. We came along after the others and we too passed the man by because we did not want to get involved. We didn't want to get involved because we just couldn't see the man for who he really was—our neighbor. Thank God the Good Samaritan stopped and assisted the man; otherwise his blood would also be on our hands.

Principle 7: CROSS EQUITY

The principle of cross equity is embedded in the phrase "the ground is level at the foot of the cross." This is true because we are all sinners before a righteous God and in need of a way of reconciliation to Him. There is no special birth rite or act of service we can render to make us righteous before God. As a result we are all in the same starting position when we come to faith in Christ. We are all equal at the foot of the cross because His suffering was not for the rich to the exclusion of the poor; not for the American to the exclusion of the Russian; not for any one brother to the exclusion of another. Christ died on that cross once for all mankind, once for all time.

As Christians we know all are equal at the cross. However, at the cross we see Christians instituting all manner of inequality. For some reason we feel compelled to find and focus on differences among the brethren. A related point is seen in the truth that we are always seen as "equal" even though we are not the "same." This could well be called the principle of equal non-sameness. The Lord has made us different so we can each play distinct parts or roles in the family. The principle of cross equity suggests we are all of equal value in the family of God. Our God is not a respecter of persons. He is not impressed with us or surprised by what we can do. If we esteem ourselves too highly may God humble us to the point of usefulness.

Principle 8: SCRATCH AND SNIFF

The scratch and sniff principle describes the need to look beneath the surface of your cross cultural interactions. Sometimes we can appear to be working well across cultures, but the reality is quite the opposite beneath the surface. Earlier I shared my experience from one of the times Karen and I lived in Cincinnati. When we scratched the surface film off the canvass of our new community we discovered the odiferous stench of racial prejudice. I call this the scratch and sniff principle because it seemed normal on the surface, but just beneath that surface was the reality of racism. Below the veneer of hospitality was a pinned up hostility. It seems we had somehow scratched the surface and released what lie beneath.

You should, from time to time, scratch the surface of your ministry and experience what lies beneath. If things look good make sure they are good. Don't ignore the responsibility of careful and critical examination. Go ahead . . . scratch and sniff.

Principle 9: TRANSPARENCY

The principle of transparency encourages leaders to candidly share information with the members of our churches and compels individuals to be open and honest in our interpersonal interactions. Transparency is a powerful deterrent to gossip and innuendo.

Sometimes our lack of transparency is rooted in a fear information will be misused. If we have had a bad experience with this as leaders it sometimes drives us to go from full disclosure to silence. The effect of this shift is creation of a perception there is something to hide. This is a weapon of the enemy. In warfare one of the rules of combat is to cut off your enemy's communications and restrict the flow of information, supplies and reinforcements to the field of battle. The devil employs this tactic in his ongoing battle against the church. Lack of transparency can sometimes be used of the devil in this same way. One of the reasons factions gathered so much steam at IBC was the previous poor flow of information and sometimes slow or inconsistent messaging from leadership on matters of importance to members. This helped to undermine leadership credibility and reduce the effectiveness of leadership's intended actions. . . Without transparency it was easy for people to imply secrecy or even deception was at work. Transparent communication helps bring people along as they share in the broader reality of the ministry.

<u>Principle 10:</u> LOYALTY LULLABY

The principle of the loyalty lullaby underscores how leaders sometimes lull their teams into an intellectual sleep by insisting they always agree with the leader. Loyalty can be a good thing. It can be an important enabler to the effective execution of any leadership post and every good leader wants a loyal following.

The problem with loyalty is it is sometimes misunderstood. Some leaders exert pressure for others to follow and support their ideas out of a sense of loyalty alone. They equate agreement to an idea with support for the leader. This is the point of departure which can make loyalty dangerous. Loyalty run amuck can set up a false dilemma where the follower feels they must retreat from their true perspective in order to appease the leader's need to always be right. In my observation, such loyalty not only sets up a false dilemma, but it can also act as a lullaby that puts the unsuspecting believer to sleep. Such loyalty can cause a person to withhold valuable input as though they were asleep during the discussion. Such input would be withheld due to the perceived risk of disagreeing with the leader.

<u>Principle 11:</u> SENSIBLE SENSITIVITY

The principle of sensible sensitivity tells how leaders should develop a heightened awareness of the needs of people. It is like the superhero characters in the old comic strips. It has become popular in our culture to make movies about these old time characters from the Marvel and DC comics of yesteryear. What made them so great? They usually had a high sense of morality and justice and they were often enabled by an incredible physical strength or a keenly heightened physical sense—ability. For example, The Daredevil was blind but could hear a pedestrian's heartbeat from atop a building. Superman could leap tall buildings in a single bound and see through objects with his unique x-ray vision. So what superhuman ability do you possess? I am uncertain whether you have any such strength or if you even need such finely tuned senses. At the same time I am convinced we could all benefit from having a more sensible sensitivity.

I learned to appreciate even more the sensibility of sensitivity. Recently I preached a sermon entitled "Close Enough to Touch." It centered on the story of Christ being touched by a woman who had been sick for twelve years. One of the amazing things about this encounter was that Jesus Christ noticed he had been touched in the first place. Think about it. He is walking in a crowd; he is moving with great intention toward an emergency situation where a little girl is dying; someone comes up behind him and touches his outer garment at the hem. And somehow Jesus notices he had been touched! I am greatly impressed by the way Jesus noticed her touch, acknowledged her faith, and met her needs. We too need to develop sensitivity to even the faintest touch of others. We too need to see the sensibility of pausing to address their needs. There is sensibility in sensitivity.

Principle 12: BALANCE

The principle of balance captures a key benefit of bringing people together in cross-cultural worship and fellowship. Balance comes when we mingle the best of the individual parts in the fairest proportion. Balance is the opposite of homogeneity. Homogeneity can often create an imbalance by composing a congregation with only one dimension or perspective. This limits the freedom of expression within the group.

Balance is what should come from integration and penetration as we engage in cross-cultural worship. Balance is the new idea. It is the idea which reflects the best of the parts but is made relevant by the whole. Balance is the new music, the new vocabulary, the new programs, the new approaches, the new ways of working which come from the melding of the separate.

This is my prayer for your ministry. I pray you will either lead or participate in a ministry with balance. I pray your ministry will have an intentional and balanced leadership team which is able to touch all aspects of the community you must reach for the Lord. I pray your leaders will do their part by being honest in personal observation of the church and allow God to do His part in reconciling us all to Himself and to each other. I pray you will balance a right perspective of proximity, cross equity, loyalty and transparency with an ability and willingness to scratch and sniff and sensibly sense beneath the surface. Remember everything ain't like it looks like it is! Don't be fooled by outward appearances. Churches all over the world are suffering terrific lack of spiritual unity, but it lies just beneath the surface. By the time the pain and suffering of division gets to the surface it is potentially fatal to the future of the ministry. Don't wait, investigate and penetrate beneath the surface of your ministry.

These are a few of the principles gleaned from all we have discussed on the preceding pages. These twelve principles are not exhaustive. I am sure you could find more principles in this text. I would love to hear from you with any additional principles you find and apply in your effort to drive cross-cultural worship. I hope this will help crystallize some of the concepts in your mind and form the basis for personal action you will take to strengthen cross-cultural worship and fellowship in your church.

CONCLUSION

We have explored, in some detail, the fallacy of affinity. In the Christian experience affinity in any form other than our common Christianity itself should never be a controlling factor. We have challenged the notion that Christian living is somehow enabled or enhanced by staying within ones own racial and ethnic affinity group. The New Testament does not suggest we stay within our affinity groups. Such notions are largely the constructs of men and are impractical in the modern era.

This is a troubling truth for some because with affinity comes comfort. In affinity-based relationships there is an ease of operating. However, just because it is easier to operate within a common racial, ethnic, gender or other affinity group, it does not mean the product of such operation is ideal. Being easier is not an indication of being better. Often the easier thing to do is in fact the wrong thing to do. I don't have to give you examples of this truth. I am sure if you thought about it for just a moment you could generate a list of examples sufficient to fill this page.

So what is the big deal? Why have I written an entire book on this subject? I wrote this book because there is a difference between what the world expects and what the Lord expects from men and women who profess Christ. The acceptable modes of operation in the world are often at significant variance from how the Christian is called to live and work and move. I wrote a book on this subject because the church in many ways is failing to acknowledge the fallacy of affinity because some of us wrongly interpret either numeric growth or the ease of comfort zone living as a proof of God's favor. I wrote this book because every believer needs to know we are called to extend ourselves beyond the limiting comforts of racial and ethnic sameness into the unlimited variety of every nation and every tongue. I wrote a book on affinity because I have been on a journey of discovery and I could not in good conscience pass the opportunity to speak on this topic.

We have presented the case for cross-cultural worship citing biblical and empirical evidence for your consideration. To fully appreciate and understand what we have discussed here it is also important to acknowledge what was not said. I did not deny affinity is a powerful force in building relationships. In worldly endeavors affinity is an effective basis for many relationships. Affinity is a key to access among professionals across many fields of endeavor. If you know the right people or simply agree with the right people, then you can often translate this into a personal advantage in this world. The ways of the world tend to strongly support nepotism, favoritism and other forms of what I call auto-centrism. Auto-centrism is self centeredness. The Bible warns against favoritism. The Apostle Paul said to Timothy, "I charge you, in the sight of God and Christ Jesus and the elect angels, to keep these instructions without partiality, and to do nothing out of favoritism."[55] The Christian life is not about being centered on ones self; rather it is about having Christ at the center of all we do. I am thoroughly convinced when we put Christ at our center we are able to fully engage across racial and ethnic barriers. With Christ as our center we are able to relate to any believer regardless of their background because we share a new and lasting commonality in Christ.

I am certain some will struggle with my premise and therefore reject the entire argument of this book. However, I might remind you what was earlier stated: this book is written to Christians. When a Christian rejects the argument for cross-cultural worship it begs many other questions. Some of those questions have been the subject of our discussion. The argument against over-emphasizing affinity is directed to those who profess Christ as Savior. I make this argument not because it is clever, but because it is consistent with New Testament teaching.

I did not say cross-cultural worship was easy, but I do propose it as a viable alternative to affinity-based churches. I invite you to join me in presenting this alternative to churches around the world. Let us break through the fallacy of affinity and so come to realize the promise of cross-cultural worship. Let us not be guilty of working against God's end game. Instead we can be a catalyst for many to experience a little taste of heavenly worship on earth. I have shared the essence of my journey with you in the hope of challenging old paradigms. I welcome the chance to learn of your journeys in cross-cultural worship. May the Lord honor our honest discussion and use it to make an impact upon the way church is done in our lifetime. In the end, should we experience any measure of success in cross-cultural worship, then I pray God will get all the glory and honor and praise.

ENDNOTES

[1] Revelation 21:1-2.

[2] Revelation 21:3.

[3] Raleigh Washington and Glen Kehrein, Breaking Down Walls: A Model for Reconciliation in an Age of Racial Strife (Chicago: Moody Press, 1993), 7.

[4] Eph. 2:14-16.

[5] Of interest, the Book of Ephesians is actually an itinerant letter. It was written by Paul to the churches of Asia Minor. In several ancient manuscripts, the phrase "at Ephesus" is not present in verse 1 of chapter 1. Many scholars agree this is left blank so Tychicus (6:21) could carry copies to each church and insert their name in this introductory section.

[6] Acts 11:26.

[7] Mark 2:14.

[8] Luke 5:27.

[9] In the original language, this phrase is spoken in the present imperative tense. Jesus impressed upon Matthew the urgency of this call to follow Him.

[10] Luke 5:28.

[11] J. Vernon McGee, Thru The Bible, (Nashville: Thomas Nelson Publishers, 1983), Vol 4, p. 389.

[12] John 4:7. New International Version.

[13] Acts 2:5-11.

[14] Acts 9:20-22.

[15] Acts 9:26.

16 Acts 22:17ff.

17 Ephesians 3:6-8.

18 What was pure or clean to eat was very clear to a Jew such as Peter according to the Old Testament tradition and law.

19 The word translated "cleanse" (2511) is to make clean in the sense of legal or ceremonial purification.

20 Acts 10:28.

21 Acts 1:8.

22 Ray Bakke, A Theology as Big as the City, (Downers Grove, IL.: InterVarsity Press, 1997). 12-13.

23 World Urbanization Prospects The 2005 Revision, Department of Economic and Social Affairs, United Nations, New York, 2006.

24 The Principal Agglomerations of the World (2007-04-21). Http://www.citypopultion.de/World.html.

25 Jim Hill and Rand Cheadle, The Bible Tells Me So: Uses and Abuses of Holy Scripture (New York: Doubleday, 1996), 3-6.

26 Matthew 22:37. This is a quote from the Old Testament passage found in Deuteronomy 6:5 which is called by the Jews, the "Shema."

27 Spiros Zodhiates, Hebrew-Greek Key Study Bible Lexical Aids to the New Testament (Chattanooga, TN: AMG Publishers, 1984), 1702.

28 Donald McGavran, Understanding Church Growth (Grand Rapids: Eardmans, 1970), 295 quoted by Harvie M. Conn, Planting and Growing Urban Churches: From Dream to Reality (Grand Rapids: Baker Books, 1997), 26.

29 2 Samuel 22:50; Psalm 18:49.

30 Deuteronomy 32:43.

31 1 Corinthians 12:21-26, New International Version.

32 My brother, Gardell, was instrumental in the development of the language of the survey questions.

33 Romans 12:16-18, New Revised Standard Version.

34 See Romans 14:13-19, New International Version.

35 See James 2:1-10, New Revised Standard Version.

36 Romans 15:7-12, New Revised Standard Version. Here the translators use the word "welcome" instead of the word "accept" we saw earlier in the NIV version of this same passage.

[37] Ephesians 2:11-13, New International Version.

[38] Ephesians 3:7-8, New International Version.

[39] Acts 2:42-47, New International Version.

[40] The pairing summary in this section provides a high-level analysis of the survey data based upon the first three survey samples.

[41] Proverbs 27:17.

[42] BASIC is an acronym for Brothers and Sisters in Christ. This is also the name of my cross-cultural ministry.

[43] He Works to Break Barriers in the Church by Karin Admiraal, The Cincinnati Post, December 9, 1998.

[44] KKK refers to a white supremacist group formally known as the Ku Klux Klan. This group was and is widely known in the US for their intense and often violent hatred of Black and Jewish people.

[45] U. S Census Bureau, Current Population Survey, 2007 Annual Social and Economic Supplement.

[46] Ibid.

[47] Monkey bread has the taste and consistency of a sweet cinnamon roll.

[48] Ephesians 4:3 and 2:17.

[49] VISION, a Weekly Publication of First Baptist Church. Volume 2, number 14. April 5, 2000.

[50] Of course God is "no respecter of persons" and I am therefore no less important in His eyes than the apostles of old. My experience, however, is perhaps an unfair comparison because Paul's Damascus revelation was a salvation experience and Peter's rooftop experience was a heaven-ordained vision.

[51] I had lived in Germany and the US, and my assignment just prior to the Singapore posting was global in scope with a focus in North America, Latin America and Western Europe.

[52] Revelation 7:9.

[53] Matthew 18:15-17.

[54] Expat is a slang term for expatriate or foreigner.

[i55] 1 Timothy 5:21.

CPSIA information can be obtained at www.ICGtesting.com
Printed in the USA
LVOW11s2317040914

402556LV00004B/98/P